**IMMIGRATION IN THE 21ST CENTURY:
POLITICAL, SOCIAL AND ECONOMIC ISSUES**

Chippewa Valley Technical College
Library
620 W. Clairemont Ave.
Eau Claire, WI 54701

IMMIGRATION VISAS

U.S. SECURITY POLICIES AND FRAUD PREVENTION

IMMIGRATION IN THE 21ST CENTURY: POLITICAL, SOCIAL AND ECONOMIC ISSUES

Additional books in this series can be found on Nova's website under the Series tab.

Additional e-books in this series can be found on Nova's website under the e-book tab.

IMMIGRATION IN THE 21ST CENTURY:
POLITICAL, SOCIAL AND ECONOMIC ISSUES

IMMIGRATION VISAS

U.S. SECURITY POLICIES AND FRAUD PREVENTION

DONALD NOWELL
EDITOR

New York

Copyright © 2014 by Nova Science Publishers, Inc.

All rights reserved. No part of this book may be reproduced, stored in a retrieval system or transmitted in any form or by any means: electronic, electrostatic, magnetic, tape, mechanical photocopying, recording or otherwise without the written permission of the Publisher.

For permission to use material from this book please contact us:
Telephone 631-231-7269; Fax 631-231-8175
Web Site: http://www.novapublishers.com

NOTICE TO THE READER

The Publisher has taken reasonable care in the preparation of this book, but makes no expressed or implied warranty of any kind and assumes no responsibility for any errors or omissions. No liability is assumed for incidental or consequential damages in connection with or arising out of information contained in this book. The Publisher shall not be liable for any special, consequential, or exemplary damages resulting, in whole or in part, from the readers' use of, or reliance upon, this material. Any parts of this book based on government reports are so indicated and copyright is claimed for those parts to the extent applicable to compilations of such works.

Independent verification should be sought for any data, advice or recommendations contained in this book. In addition, no responsibility is assumed by the publisher for any injury and/or damage to persons or property arising from any methods, products, instructions, ideas or otherwise contained in this publication.

This publication is designed to provide accurate and authoritative information with regard to the subject matter covered herein. It is sold with the clear understanding that the Publisher is not engaged in rendering legal or any other professional services. If legal or any other expert assistance is required, the services of a competent person should be sought. FROM A DECLARATION OF PARTICIPANTS JOINTLY ADOPTED BY A COMMITTEE OF THE AMERICAN BAR ASSOCIATION AND A COMMITTEE OF PUBLISHERS.

Additional color graphics may be available in the e-book version of this book.

Library of Congress Cataloging-in-Publication Data

ISBN: 978-1-63321-970-0

Published by Nova Science Publishers, Inc. † New York

CONTENTS

Preface		vii
Chapter 1	Immigration: Visa Security Policies *Ruth Ellen Wasem*	1
Chapter 2	Border Security: State Could Enhance Visa Fraud Prevention by Strategically Using Resources and Training *United States Government Accountability Office*	27
Index		71

PREFACE

This book examines visa security policies, as well as countries and visa categories that are subject to the most fraud; State's use of technologies and resources to combat fraud; and training requirements of State officials responsible for fraud prevention.

Chapter 1 - The visa issuance process is widely recognized as an integral part of immigration control and border security. Foreign nationals (i.e., aliens) not already legally residing in the United States who wish to come to the United States generally must obtain a visa to be admitted. The foreign national must establish that he/she is qualified for the visa under one of the various admission criteria. He or she must also establish that he/she is not ineligible for the visa due to one or more of the legal bars to admission. Applying for a visa is the first gateway for foreign nationals to seek admission to the United States, and the data collected as part of that process forms the core of the biometric and associated biographic data that the United States collects on foreign nationals.

The visa applicant is required to submit his or her photograph and fingerprints, as well as full name (and any other name used or by which he or she has been known), age, gender, and the date and place of birth. Depending on the visa category, certain documents must be certified by the proper government authorities (e.g., birth certificates and marriage licenses). All prospective lawful permanent residents (LPRs) must submit to physical and mental examinations, and prospective nonimmigrants also may be required to have physical and mental examinations.

Consular officers use the Consular Consolidated Database (CCD), a biometric and biographic database, to screen visa applicants. Records of all visa applications are now automated in the CCD, with some records dating back to the mid-1990s. Since February 2001, the CCD has stored photographs of all visa applicants in electronic form; since 2007, the CCD has begun storing 10- finger scans. The system links with other databases to flag problems that may have an impact on the issuance of the visa. For some years, consular officers have been required to check the background of all aliens in the "lookout" databases, specifically the Consular Lookout and Support System (CLASS) database, which contained over 42.5 million records in 2012. Consular officers use name-searching algorithms to ensure matches between names of visa applicants and any derogatory information contained in CLASS.

At its core, visa integrity protects the United States from foreign nationals who threaten public health and safety or national security, while at the same time welcomes legitimate foreign nationals who bolster the U.S. economy and foster international exchanges. Balancing these dual, and some would say competing, missions is an ongoing challenge. The policy questions center on the efficacy of the process, the security features of the policies, and whether the law needs to be revised to improve efficiency and strengthen security.

Chapter 2 - Foreign nationals may apply for entry into the United States under dozens of different visa categories, depending on circumstances. State's Bureaus of Consular Affairs and Diplomatic Security share responsibility for the prevention of visa fraud, which is a serious problem that threatens the integrity of the process. Some applicants commit fraud to obtain travel documents through illegal means, such as using counterfeit identity documents or making false claims to an adjudicating officer. Visa fraud may facilitate illegal activities in the United States, including crimes of violence, human trafficking, and terrorism. This report examines (1) countries and visa categories that are subject to the most fraud; (2) State's use of technologies and resources to combat fraud; and (3) training requirements of State officials responsible for fraud prevention. GAO examined State's reports and data on fraud trends and statistics, examined resources and technologies to counter fraud, and observed visa operations and fraud prevention efforts overseas and domestically.

In: Immigration Visas
Editor: Donald Nowell

ISBN: 978-1-63321-970-0
© 2014 Nova Science Publishers, Inc.

Chapter 1

IMMIGRATION: VISA SECURITY POLICIES[*]

Ruth Ellen Wasem

SUMMARY

The visa issuance process is widely recognized as an integral part of immigration control and border security. Foreign nationals (i.e., aliens) not already legally residing in the United States who wish to come to the United States generally must obtain a visa to be admitted. The foreign national must establish that he/she is qualified for the visa under one of the various admission criteria. He or she must also establish that he/she is not ineligible for the visa due to one or more of the legal bars to admission. Applying for a visa is the first gateway for foreign nationals to seek admission to the United States, and the data collected as part of that process forms the core of the biometric and associated biographic data that the United States collects on foreign nationals.

The visa applicant is required to submit his or her photograph and fingerprints, as well as full name (and any other name used or by which he or she has been known), age, gender, and the date and place of birth. Depending on the visa category, certain documents must be certified by the proper government authorities (e.g., birth certificates and marriage licenses). All prospective lawful permanent residents (LPRs) must submit to physical and mental examinations, and prospective nonimmigrants also may be required to have physical and mental examinations.

---

[*] This is an edited, reformatted and augmented version of a Congressional Research Service publication, No. R43589, dated June 9, 2014.

Consular officers use the Consular Consolidated Database (CCD), a biometric and biographic database, to screen visa applicants. Records of all visa applications are now automated in the CCD, with some records dating back to the mid-1990s. Since February 2001, the CCD has stored photographs of all visa applicants in electronic form; since 2007, the CCD has begun storing 10- finger scans. The system links with other databases to flag problems that may have an impact on the issuance of the visa. For some years, consular officers have been required to check the background of all aliens in the "lookout" databases, specifically the Consular Lookout and Support System (CLASS) database, which contained over 42.5 million records in 2012. Consular officers use name-searching algorithms to ensure matches between names of visa applicants and any derogatory information contained in CLASS.

At its core, visa integrity protects the United States from foreign nationals who threaten public health and safety or national security, while at the same time welcomes legitimate foreign nationals who bolster the U.S. economy and foster international exchanges. Balancing these dual, and some would say competing, missions is an ongoing challenge. The policy questions center on the efficacy of the process, the security features of the policies, and whether the law needs to be revised to improve efficiency and strengthen security.

INTRODUCTION

The visa issuance process is widely recognized as an integral part of immigration control and border security. Foreign nationals (i.e., aliens) not already legally residing in the United States who wish to come to the United States generally must obtain a visa to be admitted.[1] The foreign national must establish that he/she is qualified for the visa under one of the various admission criteria. He or she must also establish that he/she is not ineligible for the visa due to one or more of the legal bars to admission. Applying for a visa is the first gateway for foreign nationals to seek admission to the United States, and the data collected as part of that process forms the core of the biometric and associated biographic data that the United States collects on foreign nationals.

Under current law, two departments—the Department of State (DOS) and the Department of Homeland Security (DHS)—play key roles in administering the law and policies on immigration visas.[2] DOS's Bureau of Consular Affairs (Consular Affairs) is responsible for issuing visas, DHS's Citizenship and Immigration Services Bureau (USCIS) is charged with approving immigrant petitions (and nonimmigrant petitions stateside), DHS's Immigration and Customs Enforcement (ICE) operates the Visa Security Program in selected embassies abroad, and DHS's Customs and Border Protection Bureau (CBP) is tasked with inspecting all people who enter the United States.

Today's visa issuance policy dates back to 1924, when Congress first passed legislation assigning consular officers with the responsibility to approve or deny visas.[3] The Immigration Act of 1924 codified a decree in 1917 as a consequence of World War I that proclaimed aliens must present certain documents as a prerequisite to entering the United States. When the Senate Committee on the Judiciary was tasked with investigating the immigration system in 1947,[4] their report offered the following observation:

> After a study of this problem, the Congress provided in the Immigration Act of 1924 for a double check of aliens by separate independent agencies of the Government, first by consular officers before the visas were issued, and by immigration officers after the aliens reached the port of entry. If a double check was essential 25 years ago to protect the United States against criminals or other undesirables, it is the opinion of the subcommittee that it is even more necessary in the present critical condition of the world to use the double check to screen aliens seeking to enter the United States.[5]

This view prevailed in 1952 when Congress codified the various statutes on immigration and nationality into the Immigration and Nationality Act of 1952 (P.L. 82-414), which remains the basis of governing law.

At its core, visa integrity protects the United States from foreign nationals who threaten public health and safety or national security, while at the same time welcomes legitimate foreign nationals who bolster the U.S. economy and foster international exchanges. Balancing these dual, and some would say competing, missions is an ongoing challenge.[6] The policy questions center on the efficacy of the process, the security features of the policies, and whether the law needs to be revised to improve efficiency and strengthen security.

The report opens with an overview of visa issuance policy. It then explains the key provisions that guide the documentary requirements and approval/disapproval process. The section on consular screening procedures includes an analysis of trends over time in denying visas. Visa revocation, a reoccurring issue of concern to Congress, and the visa security program are discussed as well.

OVERVIEW ON VISA ISSUANCES

There are two broad classes of aliens that are issued visas: immigrants and nonimmigrants. Humanitarian admissions, such as asylees, refugees, parolees and other aliens granted relief from deportation, are handled separately under the Immigration and Nationality Act (INA). Persons granted asylum or refugee status are ultimately eligible to become legal permanent residents (LPRs).[7] Illegal aliens or unauthorized aliens include those noncitizens who entered the United States without an official inspection at a port of entry, entered with fraudulent documents, or who violated the terms of their visas after entering the United States.

Immigrant Visas

Aliens who wish to come to live permanently in the United States must meet a set of criteria specified in the INA. They must qualify as

- a spouse or minor child of a U.S. citizen;
- a parent, adult child, or sibling of an adult U.S. citizen;
- a spouse or minor child of a legal permanent resident;
- an employee that a U.S. employer has gotten approval from the Department of Labor to hire;
- a person of extraordinary or exceptional ability in specified areas;
- a refugee or asylee determined to be fleeing persecution;
- winner of a visa in the diversity lottery; or
- a person having met other specialized provisions of law.[8]

Petitions for immigrant (i.e., LPR) status are first filed with USCIS by the sponsoring relative or employer in the United States. If the prospective immigrant is already residing in the United States, the USCIS handles the entire process, which is called "adjustment of status." If the prospective LPR does not have legal residence in the United States, the petition is forwarded to Consular Affairs in their home country after USCIS has reviewed it. The Consular Affairs officer (when the alien is coming from abroad) and USCIS adjudicator (when the alien is adjusting status in the United States) must be satisfied that the alien is entitled to the immigrant status.

Nonimmigrant Visas

Aliens seeking to come to the United States temporarily rather than to live permanently are known as nonimmigrants.[9] These aliens are admitted to the United States for a temporary period of time and for an expressed reason. There are 24 major nonimmigrant visa categories, and over 70 specific types of nonimmigrant visas are issued currently. Most of these nonimmigrant visa categories are defined in §101(a)(15) of the INA. These visa categories are commonly referred to by the letter and numeral that denotes their subparagraph in §101(a)(15), e.g., B-2 tourists, F-1 foreign students, H-1B temporary professional workers, or J-1 cultural exchange participants.

Most visitors, however, enter the United States without nonimmigrant visas through the Visa Waiver Program (VWP). This provision of the INA allows the Attorney General to waive the visa documentary requirements for aliens coming as visitors from 38 countries. Since aliens entering through VWP do not have visas, CBP inspectors at the port of entry perform the background checks and admissibility reviews.[10]

KEY PROVISIONS

The documentary requirements for visas are stated in §§221-222 of the INA, with some discretion for further specifications or exceptions by regulation. Generally, the application requirements are more extensive for aliens who wish to permanently live in the United States than those coming for visits. The amount of paperwork required and the length of adjudication process to obtain a visa to come to the United States are analogous to that of the Internal Revenue Service's (IRS's) tax forms and review procedures. Just as persons with uncomplicated earnings and expenses may file an IRS "short form" while those whose financial circumstances are more complex may file a series of IRS forms, so too an alien whose situation is straightforward and whose reason for seeking a visa is easily documented generally has fewer forms and procedural hurdles than an alien whose circumstances are more complex. The visa application files must be stored in an electronic database that is available to immigration adjudicators and immigration officers in DHS.

There are over 70 U.S. Citizenship and Immigration Services (USCIS) forms as well as DOS forms that pertain to the visa issuance process.

The visa issuance procedures delineated in the statute require the petitioner to submit his or her photograph, as well as full name (and any other name used or by which he or she has been known), age, gender, and the date and place of birth. Depending on the visa category, certain documents must be certified by the proper government authorities (e.g., birth certificates and marriage licenses). All prospective LPRs must submit to physical and mental examinations, and prospective nonimmigrants also may be required to have physical and mental examinations.

§221(g) Disqualification

The statutory provision that gives the consular officer the authority to disqualify a visa applicant is broad and straightforward:

> No visa or other documentation shall be issued to an alien if (1) it appears to the consular officer, from statements in the application, or in the papers submitted therewith, that such alien is ineligible to receive a visa or such other documentation under section 212 [8 USC §1182], or any other provision of law, (2) the application fails to comply with the provisions of this Act, or the regulations issued there under, or (3) the consular officer knows or has reason to believe that such alien is ineligible to receive a visa or such other documentation under section 212 [8 USC §1182], or any other provision of law....[11]

These determinations are based on the eligibility criteria of the various and numerous visa categories.[12] The shorthand reference for these disqualifications is §221(g), which is the subsection of the INA that provides the authority.

A §221(g) disqualification is generally the most common reason an LPR visa is denied. DOS disqualified 312,968 LPR visas in FY2011 and 303,166 LPR visas in FY2012. In terms of nonimmigrant visas, DOS disqualified 837,477 visas in FY2011 and 806,773 visas in FY2012.[13]

§214(b) Presumption

Overwhelmingly, the most common reason that DOS denies nonimmigrant visas is the "failure to establish entitlement to nonimmigrant status." Specifically, §214(b) of the INA generally presumes that all aliens seeking admission to the United States are coming to live permanently; as a result, most aliens seeking a nonimmigrant visa must demonstrate that they are not coming to reside permanently.[14] DOS denied 1.2 million nonimmigrant visas in FY2011 and 1.3 million nonimmigrant visas in FY2012 on the basis of INA §214(b).[15]

§212(a) Exclusion

In addition to the determination that a foreign national is qualified for a visa, a decision must be made as to whether the foreign national is admissible or excludable under the INA. The grounds for inadmissibility are spelled out in §212(a) of the INA. These INA §212(a) inadmissibility criteria are

- health-related grounds,[16]
- criminal history,[17]
- security and terrorist concerns,[18]
- public charge (e.g., indigence),[19]
- seeking to work without proper labor certification,[20]
- illegal entrants and immigration law violations,
- ineligible for citizenship, and
- aliens previously removed.

In some cases, the foreign national may be successful in overcoming the §212(a) exclusion if new or additional information comes forward. The decision of the consular officer, however, is not subject to judicial appeals.[21]

Consular Screening Procedures

Foreign nationals seeking visas must undergo admissibility reviews performed by DOS consular officers abroad.[22] The visa applicant is required to submit his or her photograph and fingerprints, as well as full name (and any other name used or by which he or she has been known), age, gender, and the date and place of birth. Depending on the visa category, certain documents must be certified by the proper government authorities (e.g., birth certificates and marriage licenses). All prospective LPRs must submit to physical and mental examinations, and prospective nonimmigrants also may be required to have physical and mental examinations. These reviews are intended to ensure that aliens are not ineligible for visas or admission under the INA §212(a) grounds for inadmissibility.

Consular officers use the Consular Consolidated Database (CCD), a biometric and biographic database, to screen all visa applicants. Over 143 million records of visa applications are now automated in the CCD, with some records dating back to the mid-1990s. Since February 2001, the CCD has stored photographs of all visa applicants in electronic form; since 2007, the CCD has begun storing 10-finger scans.[23] The number of visa cases in the CCD surpassed 100 million in 2009, including 75 million photographs.[24]

In addition to indicating the outcome of any prior visa application of the alien in the CCD and comments by consular officers, the system links with other databases to flag problems that may have an impact on the issuance of the visa. These databases linked with the CCD include DHS's Automated Biometric Identification System (IDENT) and the Federal Bureau of Investigation (FBI) Integrated Automated Fingerprint Identification System (IAFIS) results, and supporting documents. In addition to performing biometric checks of the fingerprints for all visa applicants, DOS uses facial recognition technology to screen visa applicants against a watchlist of photos of known and suspected terrorists obtained from the Terrorist Screening Center (TSC), as well as the entire gallery of visa applicant photos contained in the CCD.

The CCD also links to the DHS's Traveler Enforcement Compliance System (TECS), a substantial database of law enforcement and border inspection information that enables CBP officers at ports of entry to have access to CCD.[25] A limited number of consular officers have been granted access to DHS' Arrival Departure Information System (ADIS).[26] ADIS tracks foreign nationals' entries into and most exits out of the United States. DOS credits access to ADIS with its ability to identify previously undetected cases of illegal overstays in the United States.[27]

Exclusion Trends[28]

As **Figure 1** shows, §212(a) denials for LPR visas have fluctuated over the past 18 years. After spiking during the FY1998-FY1999 years, they declined during the FY2000-FY2003 period. Subsequently they increased during the FY2009-FY2012 period, then dropped in FY2013. In terms of nonimmigrants, §212(a) denials have exhibited a slower, but steadier upward trend during the period examined.

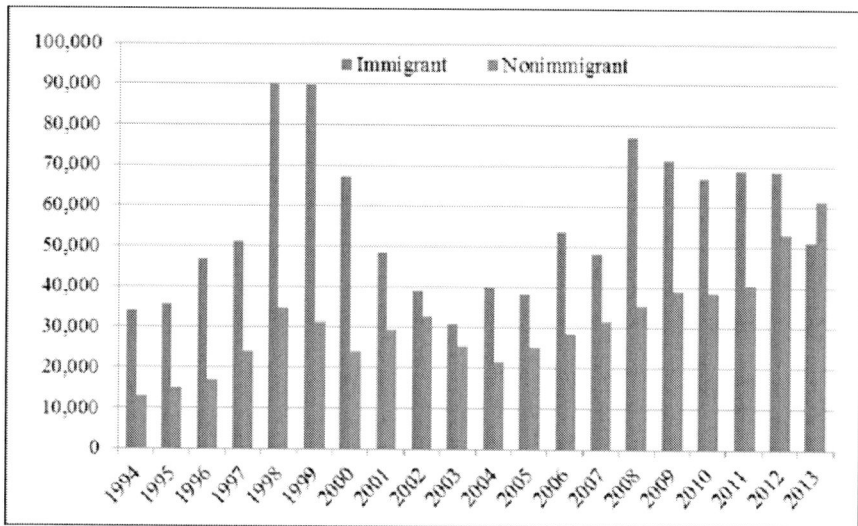

Source: CRS presentation of initial determination data from Table XX of the annual reports of the U.S. Department of State, Office of Visa Statistics (multiple years).
Notes: FY2013 data is preliminary. Data are initial determinations of inadmissibility. Some denials may be overcome with additional evidence.

Figure 1. Aliens Denied Visas Under §212(a) Inadmissibility; FY1994 through FY2013.

Public charge exclusions accounted for the spike during the period immediately after passage of the Illegal Immigration Reform and Immigrant Responsibility Act (IIRIRA) of 1996 (Division C of P.L. 104-208), as depicted in **Figure 2**. IIRIRA had strengthened the enforceability of the inadmissibility provisions aimed at indigent or low-income people.[29] Public charge exclusions dominated inadmissibility for LPRs until the FY2003-FY2005 period.

Since FY2008, prior removals/illegal presence has become the top single ground of inadmissibility. IIRIRA had ramped up the consequences for foreign nationals attempting to return to the United States if they had prior orders of removal or had been illegally present in the United States, and the databases monitoring such violations improved over the years. The failure of some employers hiring foreign workers to meet the labor certification ground consistently ranked third over the period examined.[30]

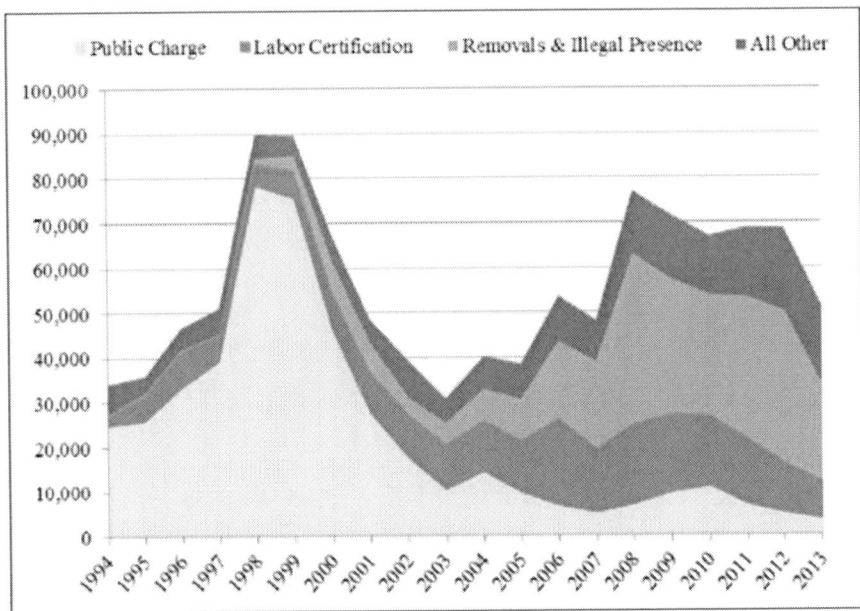

Source: CRS presentation of initial determination data from Table XX of the annual reports of the U.S. Department of State, Office of Visa Statistics (multiple years).

Notes: FY2013 data is preliminary. Data are initial determinations of inadmissibility. Some denials may be overcome with additional evidence.

Figure 2. Prospective LPRs Denied Visas by Major §212(a) Inadmissibility Grounds; FY1994 through FY2013.

In terms of nonimmigrants, prior removals/illegal presence has also become the top single ground of inadmissibility; however, the grounds for excluding nonimmigrants have otherwise exhibited a different pattern than that of immigrant exclusions. Two grounds less commonly cited for immigrant exclusions—criminal history and INA violations—have been frequent grounds for denying nonimmigrant visas.

As **Figure 3** shows, criminal history has been a leading basis of nonimmigrant exclusion. The preliminary FY2013 data[31] indicate that prior removals/illegal presence comprised 39% of the basis of nonimmigrant exclusions and criminal history made up 26% of the basis of nonimmigrant exclusions. In contrast, criminal history comprised only 4% of *immigrant* exclusions in FY2013 and was too small to depict. Another top basis of excluding nonimmigrants has been INA violations, i.e., nonimmigrants who sought to procure or had procured either admission into the United States or a benefit under the INA by fraud or willful misrepresentation of a material fact.[32] This latter ground had been the most common basis for nonimmigrant exclusion in the late 1990s, as **Figure 3** depicts.[33]

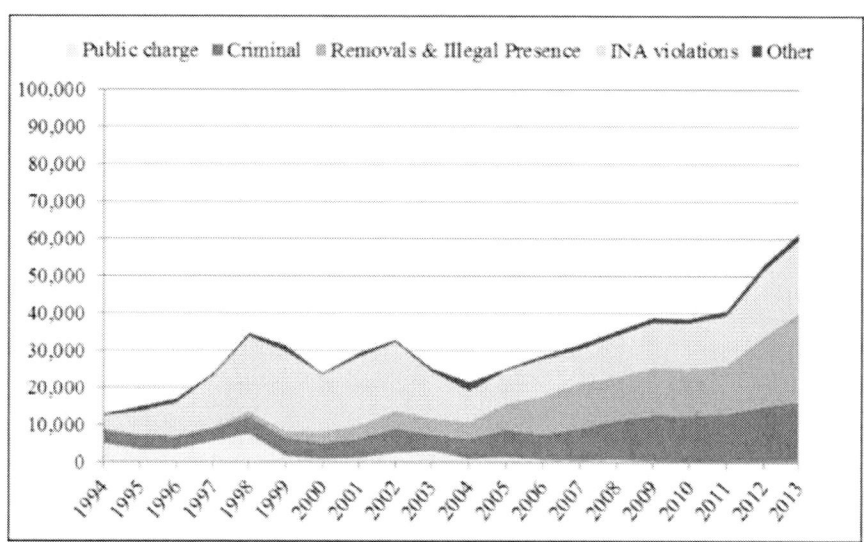

Source: CRS presentation of initial determination data from Table XX of the annual reports of the U.S. Department of State, Office of Visa Statistics (multiple years).
Notes: FY2013 data is preliminary. Data are initial determinations of inadmissibility. Some denials may be overcome with additional evidence. "INA violations" as depicted here have largely been those of misrepresentation under INA §212(a)(6).

Figure 3. Prospective Nonimmigrants Denied Visas by Major §212(a) Inadmissibility Grounds; FY1994 through FY2013.

National Security and Public Safety Reviews

For some years, consular officers have been required to check the background of all aliens in the "lookout" databases.[34] DOS specifically uses the Consular Lookout and Support System (CLASS) database, which contained over 42.5 million records in 2012. Consular officers use name-searching algorithms to ensure matches between names of visa applicants and any derogatory information contained in CLASS. DOS reports that about 70% of the records in CLASS come from other agencies, including DHS, the FBI, and the Drug Enforcement Administration (DEA). DOS also employs an automated CLASS search algorithm that runs the names of all visa applicants against the CCD to check for any prior visa applications, refusals, or issuances.[35]

DOS has relied on the Security Advisory Opinion (SAO) system, which requires a consular officer abroad to refer selected visa cases for greater review by intelligence and law enforcement agencies.[36] The current interagency procedures for alerting officials about foreign nationals who may be suspected terrorists, referred to in State Department nomenclature as Visa Viper, began after the 1993 World Trade Center bombing and were institutionalized by enactment of the Enhanced Border Security and Visa Entry Reform Act of 2002. If consular officials receive information about a foreign national that causes concern, they send a Visa Viper cable (which is a dedicated and secure communication) to the National Counterterrorism Center (NCTC).

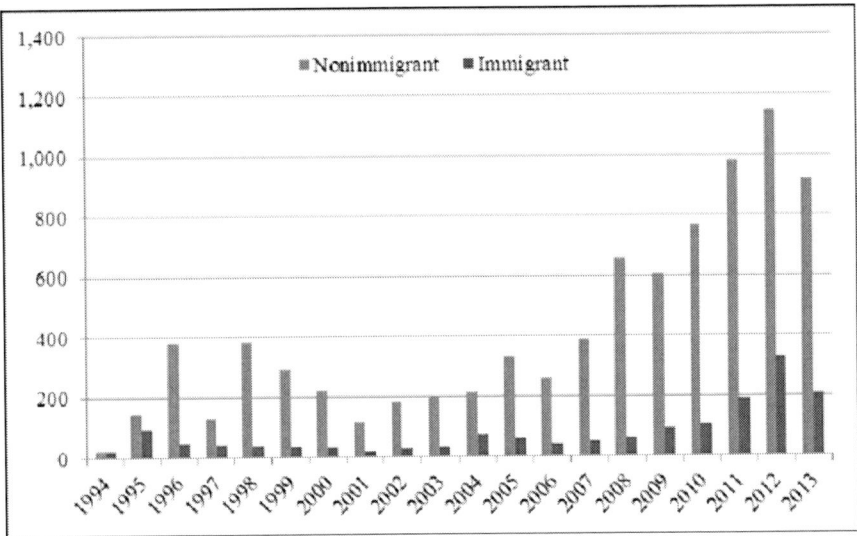

Source: CRS presentation of initial determination data from Table XX of the annual reports of the U.S. Department of State, Office of Visa Statistics (multiple years).

Notes: FY2013 data is preliminary. Data are initial determinations of inadmissibility. Some denials may be overcome with additional evidence. The primary axis scale here is set at 1,400 (rather than 100,000 of the Figures 1-3) to better illustrate the trends.

Figure 4. Aliens Denied Visas Under Terrorist Grounds of Inadmissibility; FY1994 through FY2013.

In a similar set of SAO procedures, consular officers send suspect names, identified by law enforcement and intelligence information, to the FBI for a name check program called Visa Condor.[37] There is also the "Terrorist Exclusion List" (TEL), which lists organizations designated as terrorist-supporting and includes the names of individuals associated with these organizations.[38]

In June 2013, DOS began "Kingfisher Expansion" (KFE) in partnership with the NCTC for conducting interagency counterterrorism screening of all visa applicants.[39] The consular official submits the visa applicants' electronic visa applications as a "vetting package" to the NCTC. In turn NCTC uses an automated process to compare the vetting package with its holdings. A "hit" in KFE triggers a Washington-based interagency review of the visa application. KFE also conducts post-issuance reviews of valid visas to check for new information on emerging threats.[40]

Despite dipping somewhat in FY2013, the number of aliens denied visas under terrorist grounds of inadmissibility has increased since the 1990s and mid-2000s. As **Figure 4** shows, this trend holds for immigrant and nonimmigrant exclusions.[41]

VISA REVOCATION

After a visa has been issued, the consular officer as well as the Secretary of State has the discretionary authority to revoke a visa at any time.[42] A consular officer must revoke a visa if

- the alien is ineligible under the INA §212(a) grounds of inadmissibility to receive such a visa, or was issued a visa and overstayed the time limits of the visa;
- the alien is not entitled to the nonimmigrant visa classification under INA §101(a)(15) definitions specified in such visa;
- the visa has been physically removed from the passport in which it was issued; or
- the alien has been issued an immigrant visa.[43]

This applies, for example, to findings of ineligibility under "misrepresentation," "terrorist activity" or "foreign policy."[44] FAM further instructs: "pending receipt of the Department's advisory opinion, the consular officer must enter the alien's name in the CLASS under a quasi-refusal code, if warranted."[45] According to DOS officials, they sometimes prudentially revoke visas (i.e., they revoke a visa as a safety precaution).[46]

When a consular officer suspects that a visa revocation may involve U.S. law enforcement interests, FAM instructs the consular officer to consult with law enforcement agencies at the consular post and inform the State officials of the case, to permit consultations with potentially interested entities before a revocation is made.[47] The rationale for this consultation is that there may be legal or intelligence investigations that would be compromised if the visa were revoked and that law enforcement and intelligence officials may prefer to monitor the individual to further investigate their actions and associates.

Visa revocation has been a ground for removal in the INA §237(a)(1)(B) since enactment of P.L. 108-458 in December 2004. This provision (§5304 of P.L. 108-458) permits limited judicial review of removal if visa revocation is the sole basis of the removal.

On April 27, 2011, the DOS promulgated regulations that broadened the revocation authority.

> (a) Grounds for revocation by consular officers. A consular officer, the Secretary, or a Department official to whom the Secretary has delegated this authority is authorized to revoke a nonimmigrant visa at any time, in his or her discretion.
>
> (b) Provisional revocation. A consular officer, the Secretary, or any Department official to whom the Secretary has delegated this authority may provisionally revoke a nonimmigrant visa while considering information related to whether a visa holder is eligible for the visa. Provisional revocation shall have the same force and effect as any other visa revocation under INA 221(i).
>
> (c) Notice of revocation. Unless otherwise instructed by the Department, a consular officer shall, if practicable, notify the alien to whom the visa was issued that the visa was revoked or provisionally revoked. Regardless of delivery of such notice, once the revocation has been entered into the Department's Consular Lookout and Support System (CLASS), the visa is no longer to be considered valid for travel to the United States. The date of the revocation shall be indicated in CLASS and on any notice sent to the alien to whom the visa was issued.
>
> (d) Procedure for physically canceling visas. A nonimmigrant visa that is revoked shall be canceled by writing or stamping the word " REVOKED" plainly across the face of the visa, if the visa is available to the consular officer. The failure or inability to physically cancel the visa does not affect the validity of the revocation.[48]

These regulations sought to address a series of concerns that have been raised in recent years about the visa revocation process, especially relating to the timely transmission of information among federal agencies.[49]

DHS VISA SECURITY PROGRAM

As discussed more fully in **Appendix**, §428 of the Homeland Security Act (HSA) gave the Secretary of DHS the authority to assign DHS employees to diplomatic and consular posts. The duties of these DHS employees were delineated in HSA §428 as

- provide expert advice and training to consular officers regarding specific security threats relating to the adjudication of individual visa applications or classes of applications;
- review any such applications, either on the initiative of DHS or upon request by a consular officer or other person charged with adjudicating such applications; and
- conduct investigations with respect to consular matters under the jurisdiction of the Secretary of DHS.

This statutory language established what is currently known as the Visa Security Program (VSP). The Immigration and Customs Enforcement (ICE) Office of International Affairs (OIA) operates the VSP in consular posts deemed to be high-risk. As described by DHS, the VSP sends ICE special agents with expertise in immigration law and counterterrorism to diplomatic posts overseas to perform visa security activities, which aim to complement the DOS visa screening process with law enforcement resources not available to consular officers.

The first VSP units were established in Saudi Arabia, as required by HSA §428. In October 2005, VSP units were set up in: Manila, Philippines; Abu Dhabi and Dubai in the United Arab Emirates; and Islamabad, Pakistan. By the end of 2007, there were VSP units in: Cairo, Egypt; Caracas, Venezuela; Montreal, Canada; Hong Kong, China; and Casablanca, Morocco.[50] There were 19 VSP units in 13 countries as of November 2013.

One of the major tasks of the VSP agents is to screen visa applicants to determine the applicant's risk profile. Unlike consular officers, VSP agents have access to DHS's Traveler Enforcement Compliance System (TECS). The ICE agent further vets visa applicants who are possible matches, performing additional research and investigation of the visa applicant (e.g., in-depth searches in law enforcement databases and other information systems, examining documents, and consulting with consular, law enforcement, or other officials).[51]

VSP agents are supposed to engage in informal discussions with consular officers, as well as develop formal, targeted training and briefings to inform consular officers and others about threats to the visa process. They "identify and monitor the threat environment and trends in the visa applicant pool specific to their post and host country.... Examples of topics covered in these briefings include fraud trends in specific visa categories and how to identify fraudulent documents and imposters."[52] Aimed at improving VSP integration in the SAO process, Congress appropriated $5 million to establish an SAO review unit within VSP headquarters in FY2007.[53]

CONGRESSIONAL ACTIVITY[54]

Since the beginning of the 113th Congress, a series of hearings have been held that discussed visa issuances and security policy. These hearings include the following:

- Senate Committee on the Judiciary hearing on the Border Security, Economic Opportunity, and Immigration Modernization Act, S. 744 (April 22, 2013)
- House Committee on Homeland Security, Subcommittee on Border and Maritime Security hearing titled "Visa Security and Overstays: How Secure is America?" (May 13, 2013)
- House Committee on the Judiciary hearing on H.R. 2278, the Strengthen and Fortify Enforcement Act (June 13, 2013)
- House Committee on Oversight and Government Reform, Subcommittee on National Security hearing on Securing the U.S. Border, B1/B2 Visas and Border Crossing Cards (November 14, 2013)

As evident from the hearing titles, the different committees explored various aspects of the issues. One piece of legislation with provisions aimed at visa security (H.R. 2278) has received action thus far in the 113th Congress.[55] The Senate-passed comprehensive immigration reform legislation, the Border Security, Economic Opportunity, and Immigration Modernization Act (S. 744) does not include provisions on visa security, but it does include provisions aimed at enhanced processing of certain visas.[56]

COMPETING CONCERNS

Some have expressed the view that DOS retains too much power and control over visa security. They maintain the Homeland Security Act of 2002 intended DHS to be the lead department and that DOS was to merely administer the visa issuances. They warn that consular officers are too concerned about facilitating tourism and trade to scrutinize visa applicants thoroughly.[57] Some argue that visa issuance is the real "front line" of homeland security against terrorists and that the principal responsibility should be in DHS, which does not have competing priorities of diplomatic relations and reciprocity with foreign governments.[58]

Others have indicated satisfaction with current law, arguing that it strikes the proper balance between the two departments and reflects the bifurcation envisioned in the act. They maintain that it plays off the strengths of the two departments and allows for refinement of the implementation in the future.[59] Proponents of DOS playing the lead role in visa issuances assert that only consular officers in the field have the country-specific knowledge to make decisions about whether an alien is admissible and that staffing 250 diplomatic and consular posts around the world would stretch DHS beyond its capacity.[60]

APPENDIX. RESPECTIVE ROLES OF THE DEPARTMENTS OF STATE AND HOMELAND SECURITY

When the 107th Congress weighed the creation of the Department of Homeland Security, considerable debate surfaced about whether or not any or all visa issuance functions should be located in the new agency. Enactment of the Homeland Security Act of 2002 (P.L. 107-293) resolved most of these issues, but concerns over the roles and responsibilities of the two departments have frequently arisen.

Immigration and Nationality Act

The powers and duties of the Secretary of State are delineated in §104 of the INA. Most significantly, §104 (a) states: "The Secretary of State shall be charged with the administration and the enforcement of the provisions of this Act and all other immigration and nationality laws relating to (1) the powers, duties and functions of diplomatic and consular officers of the United States, *except those powers, duties and functions conferred upon the consular officers relating to the granting or refusal of visas;....* "[61] The INA specifically gives consular officers the sole authority to issue visas in §221 of the act.[62] Over the years, the courts have held that consular decisions are not appealable.[63] Under proscribed circumstances, the Secretary of State may direct a consular officer to deny a visa to a particular inadmissible alien.[64]

Enhanced Border Security and Visa Entry Reform Act of 2002

After the terrorist attacks on September 11, 2001, Congress enacted the Enhanced Border Security and Visa Entry Reform Act of 2002 (P.L. 107-173), which aimed to improve the visa issuance process abroad, as well as immigration inspections at the border. It expressly increased consular officers' access to electronic information needed for alien screening. Specifically, it required the development of an interoperable electronic data system to be used to share information relevant to alien admissibility and removability and the implementation of an integrated entry-exit data system. It also required that all visas issued by October 2004 have biometric identifiers.[65] In addition to increasing consular officers' access to electronic information needed for visa issuances, it expanded the training requirements for consular officers who issue visas.

§428 of the Homeland Security Act of 2002

The Homeland Security Act of 2002 (HSA) contained language stating that DHS is responsible for formulating regulations on visa issuances. In §428, the Secretary of DHS is expressly tasked as follows:

> ... shall be vested exclusively with all authorities to issue regulations with respect to, administer, and enforce the provisions of such Act,

and of all other immigration and nationality laws, relating to the functions of consular officers of the United States in connection with the granting or refusal of visas, and shall have the authority to refuse visas in accordance with law and to develop programs of homeland security training for consular officers (in addition to consular training provided by the Secretary of State), which authorities shall be exercised through the Secretary of State, *except that the Secretary shall not have authority to alter or reverse the decision of a consular officer to refuse a visa to an alien....* [66]

The HSA also enabled DHS to assign staff to consular posts abroad to advise, review, and conduct investigations, which is discussed more fully below. It further stated that DOS's Consular Affairs continued to be responsible for issuing visas. The HSA required DHS and DOS to reach an understanding on how the details of this division of responsibilities would be implemented.[67]

2003 Memorandum of Understanding

On September 28, 2003, then-Secretary of State Colin Powell and then-Secretary of Homeland Security Thomas Ridge signed the memorandum of understanding (MOU) implementing §428 of the HSA. The MOU described each department's responsibilities in the area of visa issuances. Among its major elements, the MOU stated that DOS may propose and issue visa regulations subject to DHS consultation and final approval. It further stated that DHS shall assign personnel to diplomatic posts, but that DOS will determine who, how many, and the scope of their functions.[68]

Then-Assistant Secretary of State for Consular Affairs Maura Harty described several key responsibilities that remain with the DOS.

> The Secretary of State will have responsibility over certain visa decisions, including decisions of a foreign policy nature.... He will also be responsible for establishing visa validity periods and fees based on reciprocity. In the case of visa validity periods, however, he will consult with Homeland Security before lengthening them, and Homeland Security will have authority to determine that certain persons or classes of persons cannot benefit from the maximum validity period for security reasons. The Secretary of State will also exercise all the foreign policy-related grounds of visa denial enumerated in Section 428 and the additional provision, not specifically enumerated, under which we deny visas to persons who have confiscated the property of American citizens without just compensation.[69]

She emphasized that the MOU "recognizes that the Secretary of State must have control over officers in his chain of command." She further stated that "DHS officers assigned visa duties abroad may provide input related to the evaluations of consular officers doing visa work, but the evaluations themselves will be written by State Department consular supervisors," and that "direction to consular officers will come from their State Department supervisors, and all officers assigned abroad, including DHS, come under the authority of the Chief of Mission."[70]

In congressional testimony during October 2003, C. Stewart Verdery, Jr., as then-DHS Assistant Secretary for Border and Transportation Security Policy and Planning, discussed DHS' role in visa security. Verdery reported that DHS officers were already in Saudi Arabia reviewing all visa applications prior to adjudication (as required by §428(i) of P.L. 107-296). He indicated that officers in Riyadh and Jeddah also provided assistance, expert advice and training to consular officers on fraudulent documents, fingerprinting techniques and identity fraud. More specifically, he stated:

> As part of the review process, DHS officers at home and abroad have full access to a variety of law enforcement databases, including the National Crime Information Center (NCIC); Treasury Enforcement Communication System (TECS); Interagency Border Inspections System (IBIS); National Security Entry Exit System (NSEERS); Student Exchange and Visitor Information System (SEVIS); Biometric 2-print fingerprint system (IDENT); and Advanced Passenger Information System (APIS). They also have access to selected legacy-INS automated adjudications data and certain commercial databases.[71]

Visa Security Program Memoranda of Understanding

Additionally, §428 of the HSA gave the Secretary of DHS the authority to assign DHS employees to diplomatic and consular posts, which became the statutory basis of the Visa Security Program (VSP). In 2004, DHS and DOS signed a MOU on administrative aspects of assigning personnel overseas as part of the VSP. Among other things, this MOU described administrative support, security, facilities, security awareness training, and information systems for VSP personnel.

On January 11, 2011, DHS and DOS signed another MOU which further delineates the roles, responsibilities, and collaboration of VSP agents, consular officers, and diplomatic security officers in daily operations of VSP at posts overseas.[72] The 2011 MOU discusses general collaboration between ICE and

State for VSP operations; roles and responsibilities of VSP agents and consular officers and routine interaction between the officers and agents; development of formal, targeted training and briefings by VSP agents for consular officers and other U.S. government officials at post; clarification of the dispute resolution process; and collaboration between diplomatic security officers and VSP agents on visa and passport fraud investigations.[73]

Intelligence Reform and Terrorism Prevention Act of 2004

Congress also relied on recommendations made by the National Commission on Terrorist Attacks Upon the United States (also known as the 9/11 Commission) to revise visa security policies. The Intelligence Reform and Terrorism Prevention Act of 2004 (P.L. 108-458) mandated improvements in technology and training to assist consular and immigration officers in detecting and combating terrorist travel. Among other provisions, it required the Secretary of Homeland Security, in consultation with the Director of the National Counter Terrorism Center, to establish a program to oversee DHS's responsibilities with respect to terrorist travel and required the Secretary of State to establish a Visa and Passport Security Program within the Bureau of Diplomatic Security at the Department of State.

The Intelligence Reform and Terrorism Prevention Act added requirements for an in-person consular interview of most applicants for nonimmigrant visas between the ages of 14 and 79. It further mandated that an alien applying for a nonimmigrant visa must completely and accurately respond to any request for information contained in his or her application.

End Notes

[1] Authorities to except or to waive visa requirements are specified in law, such as the broad parole authority of the Attorney General under §212(d)(5) of Immigration and Nationality Act (INA) and the specific authority of the Visa Waiver Program in §217 of INA. CRS Report RL32221, *Visa Waiver Program*, by Alison Siskin.

[2] Other departments, notably the Department of Labor (DOL), and the Department of Agriculture (USDA), play roles in the approval process depending on the category or type of visa sought, and the Department of Health and Human Services (DHHS) sets policy on the health-related grounds for inadmissibility discussed below. The Department of Justice's Executive Office for Immigration Review (EOIR) has a significant policy role through its adjudicatory decisions on specific immigration cases.

[3] Immigration Act of May 26, 1924; 43 Stat. 153.

[4] During the 80th Congress, Senate Resolution 137, which passed on July 26, 1947, directed the Senate Committee on the Judiciary to make a full and complete investigation of the entire immigration system.

[5] U.S. Congress, Senate Committee on the Judiciary, *The Immigration and Naturalization Systems of the United States, report pursuant to S. Res.137*, committee print, 81st Cong., 2nd sess., April 20, 1950.

[6] These goals are comparable to the twofold mission of the CBP port-of-entry border inspections process. For further discussion of border inspections, see CRS Report R43356, *Border Security: Immigration Inspections at Ports of Entry*, by Lisa Seghetti.

[7] For background and further discussion of humanitarian cases, see CRS Report RL31269, *Refugee Admissions and Resettlement Policy*, by Andorra Bruno, and CRS Report RS20844, *Temporary Protected Status: Current Immigration Policy and Issues*, by Ruth Ellen Wasem and Karma Ester.

[8] For a more complete discussion of LPR categories and a statistical analysis of admissions trends, see CRS Report R42866, *Permanent Legal Immigration to the United States: Policy Overview*, by Ruth Ellen Wasem.

[9] For a full discussion and analysis of nonimmigrant visas, see CRS Report RL31381, *U.S. Immigration Policy on Temporary Admissions*, by Ruth Ellen Wasem. (Hereinafter cited as RL31381, *Temporary Admissions*.)

[10] CRS Report RL32221, *Visa Waiver Program*, by Alison Siskin.

[11] Section 221(g) of the INA. 8 U.S.C. 1201.

[12] For further information and analysis of these numerous visa categories, see CRS Report RL32235, *U.S. Immigration Policy on Permanent Admissions*, by Ruth Ellen Wasem, and CRS Report RL31381, *Temporary Admissions*.

[13] Bureau of Consular Affairs, *Report of the Visa Office 2012*, U.S. Department of State, Table XX, 2013; and Bureau of Consular Affairs, *Report of the Visa Office 2011*, U.S. Department of State, Table XX, 2012.

[14] §214(b) of the INA; 8 U.S.C. §1184(b). There are three nonimmigrant visas that might be considered provisional in that the visaholder may simultaneously seek LPR status. As a result, the law exempts nonimmigrants seeking any one of these three visas, i.e., H-1 professional workers, L intracompany transfers, and V accompanying family members, from the requirement that they prove they are not coming to live permanently.

[15] Bureau of Consular Affairs, *Report of the Visa Office 2012*, U.S. Department of State, Table XX, 2013; and Bureau of Consular Affairs, *Report of the Visa Office 2011*, U.S. Department of State, Table XX, 2012.

[16] For further discussion, see CRS Report R40570, *Immigration Policies and Issues on Health-Related Grounds for Exclusion*, by Ruth Ellen Wasem.

[17] For further discussion, see CRS Report RL32480, *Immigration Consequences of Criminal Activity*, by Michael John Garcia.

[18] For further discussion, see CRS Report RL32564, *Immigration: Terrorist Grounds for Exclusion and Removal of Aliens*, by Michael John Garcia and Ruth Ellen Wasem.

[19] For further discussion, see CRS Report R43220, *Public Charge Grounds of Inadmissibility and Deportability: Legal Overview*, by Kate M. Manuel.

[20] For further discussion, see CRS Report R43223, *The Framework for Foreign Workers' Labor Protections Under Federal Law*, by Margaret Mikyung Lee and Jon O. Shimabukuro; and CRS Report RL33977, *Immigration of Foreign Workers: Labor Market Tests and Protections*, by Ruth Ellen Wasem.

[21] For more complete discussion of INA §212(a), see CRS Report R41104, *Immigration Visa Issuances and Grounds for Exclusion: Policy and Trends*, by Ruth Ellen Wasem.

[22] USCIS adjudicators also conduct admissibility reviews for petitions filed within the United States, and CBP inspectors do so when aliens seek entry to the United States.

[23] Consular officers transmit the fingerprints taken during the visa process to CBP officers at ports of entry, enabling them to match the fingerprints of persons entering the United States.

[24] Margaret P. Grafeld, Department of State Privacy Coordinator, *Consular Consolidated Database (CCD) Privacy Impact Assessment (PIA)*, U.S. Department of State, March 22, 2010.

[25] Consular officers do not have direct access to the TECS database.

[26] Unclassified congressional staff briefing by Assistant Secretary of State Janice Jacobs, January 11, 2010.

[27] CRS Report RS22446, *Nonimmigrant Overstays: Brief Synthesis of the Issue*, by Ruth Ellen Wasem.

[28] For a more complete analysis of exclusion trends, see CRS Report R41104, *Immigration Visa Issuances and Grounds for Exclusion: Policy and Trends*, by Ruth Ellen Wasem.

[29] For further discussion, see CRS Report R43220, *Public Charge Grounds of Inadmissibility and Deportability: Legal Overview*, by Kate M. Manuel.

[30] Bureau of Consular Affairs, *Report of the Visa Office*, U.S. Department of State, Table XX (multiple years).

[31] DOS Office of Visa Statistics states that "Fiscal Year 2013 data is preliminary and is subject to change. Any changes would not be statistically significant." http://travel.state.

[32] INA §212(a)(6).

[33] Bureau of Consular Affairs, *Report of the Visa Office*, U.S. Department of State, Table XX (multiple years).

[34] Lookout databases store information on persons whose entry might pose a threat to the safety or security of the United States.

[35] U.S. Congress, House Committee on Homeland Security, Subcommittee on Border and Maritime Security, *From the 9/11 Hijackers to Amine El-Khalifi: Terrorists and the Visa Overstay Problem*, testimony of David T. Donahue, Deputy Assistant Secretary for Visa Services, 112th Cong., 2nd sess., March 6, 2012.

[36] U.S. Congress, Senate Committee on Foreign Relations, Subcommittee on International Operations and Terrorism, *The Post 9/11 Visa Reforms and New Technology: Achieving the Necessary Security Improvements in a Global Environment*, hearing, October 23, 2003.

[37] U.S. Congress, Senate Committee on Foreign Relations, Subcommittee on International Operations and Terrorism, *The Post 9/11 Visa Reforms and New Technology: Achieving the Necessary Security Improvements in a Global Environment*, hearing, October 23, 2003.

[38] For further discussion of terrorist screening, see CRS Report RL32564, *Immigration: Terrorist Grounds for Exclusion and Removal of Aliens*, by Michael John Garcia and Ruth Ellen Wasem.

[39] KFE also coordinates with DHS (including CBP and U.S. Immigration and Customs Enforcement (ICE), the FBI, and the FBI's Terrorist Screening Center.

[40] U.S. Congress, House Committee on Oversight and Government Reform, Subcommittee on National Security, *Hearing on Securing the U.S. Border, B1/B2 Visas and Border Crossing Cards*, testimony of Edward J. Ramotowski, Deputy Assistant Secretary for Visa Services, 113th Cong., 1st sess., November 14, 2013.

[41] Bureau of Consular Affairs, *Report of the Visa Office*, U.S. Department of State, Table XX (multiple years).

[42] §221(i) of the INA; 8 U.S.C. §1201(i); §1201(i); 9 FAM 41.122 N1.
[43] 9 F.A.M. §41.122 Notes N1.
[44] Testimony of Janice L. Jacobs, Deputy Assistant Secretary of State for Visa Services, in U.S. Congress, Senate Committee on the Judiciary, Subcommittee on Immigration, Border Security and Citizenship, *Visa Issuance, Information Sharing and Enforcement in a Post-9/11 Environment: Are We Ready Yet?* hearing, July 15, 2003.
[45] 22 C.F.R. §41.122 Notes PN3.
[46] Testimony of Janice L. Jacobs, Deputy Assistant Secretary of State for Visa Services, in U.S. Congress, Senate Committee on the Judiciary, Subcommittee on Immigration, Border Security and Citizenship, *Visa Issuance, Information Sharing and Enforcement in a Post-9/11 Environment: Are We Ready Yet?* hearing, July 15, 2003.
[47] 22 C.F.R. §41.122 Notes PN9.2-1.
[48] U.S. Department of State, "Visas: Documentation of Nonimmigrants Under the Immigration and Nationality Act, As Amended," 76 *Federal Register* 23477-23479, April 27, 2011.
[49] For examples of past critiques, see U.S. General Accounting Office, *New Policies and Procedures Are Needed to Fill Gaps in the Visa Revocation Process*, GAO 03-798, June 18, 2003; and U.S. General Accounting Office, *Border Security: Additional Actions Needed to Eliminate Weaknesses in the Visa Revocation Process*, GAO-04-795, July 13, 2004.
[50] Office of Inspector General, *U.S. Immigration and Customs Enforcement Visa Security Program*, U.S. Department of Homeland Security, July 2008. (Hereafter OIG, *Visa Security Program*, July 2008.)
[51] OIG, *Visa Security Program*, July 2008.
[52] OIG, *Visa Security Program*, July 2008.
[53] House and Senate Committees on Appropriations, "Summary of the Fiscal 2007 Supplemental Funding Legislation," press release, April 23, 2007.
[54] For legislative tracking of the major immigration bills, see CRS Report R43320, *Immigration Legislation and Issues in the 113th Congress*, coordinated by Andorra Bruno.
[55] For a legal analysis of this legislation, see CRS Report R43192, *Immigration Enforcement: Major Provisions in H.R. 2278, the Strengthen and Fortify Enforcement Act (SAFE Act)*, by Michael John Garcia and Kate M. Manuel.
[56] For a discussion of these provisions, see CRS Report R43097, *Comprehensive Immigration Reform in the 113th Congress: Major Provisions in Senate-Passed S. 744*, by Ruth Ellen Wasem, pp. 50-51.
[57] Proponents of this view often cite Office of Inspector General, *Review of Nonimmigrant Visa Issuance Policy and Procedures*, U.S. Department of State, Memorandum Report ISP-I-03-26, December 2002, http://oig.state.gov/ documents/organization/16215.pdf.
[58] Former Senator Joseph Lieberman appearing on ABC's "This Week," January 3, 2010.
[59] U.S. Congress, Senate Committee on the Judiciary, *Securing America's Safety: Improving the Effectiveness of Anti-Terrorism Tools and Inter-Agency Communication*, Statement of Senator Patrick Leahy, 111th Cong., 2nd sess., January 20, 2010.
[60] Proponents of this view often cite the conclusions of this report: U.S. Government Accountability Office, *Strengthened Visa Process Would Benefit from Improvements in Staffing and Information Sharing*, GAO-05-859, September, 2005.
[61] 8 U.S.C. 1104.
[62] 8 U.S.C. 1201.
[63] Some critics of transferring the visa function to DHS warned that visa issuance "adjudication" might become subject to judicial appeals or other due process considerations if a stateside agency, such as DHS, assumed responsibility. As a result, §428(f) of the HSA stated:

"Nothing in this section shall be construed to create or authorize a private right of action to challenge a decision of a consular officer or other United States official or employee to grant or deny a visa."

[64] §428(c) of the Homeland Security Act of 2002 (P.L. 107-296).

[65] DOS met the 2004 deadline for biometric visas.

[66] §428 (b)(1) of the Homeland Security Act (P.L. 107-296).

[67] For a complete account of this debate, see CRS Report R41093, *Visa Security Policy: Roles of the Departments of State and Homeland Security*, by Ruth Ellen Wasem.

[68] Colin L. Powell and Thomas J. Ridge, *Memorandum of Understanding between the Secretaries of State and Homeland Security Concerning the Implementation of Section 428 of the Homeland Security Act of 2002*, September 29, 2003.

[69] U.S. Congress, Senate Committee on the Judiciary, Subcommittee On Immigration, Border Security and Citizenship, *Visa Issuance: Our First Line of Defense for Homeland Security*, hearing, September 30, 2003.

[70] Ibid.

[71] U.S. Congress, Senate Committee on Foreign Relations, Subcommittee on International Operations and Terrorism, *The Post 9/11 Visa Reforms and New Technology: Achieving the Necessary Security Improvements in a Global Environment*, hearing, Oct. 23, 2003.

[72] *Memorandum of Understanding Among U.S. Immigration and Customs Enforcement of the Department of Homeland Security and the Bureau of Consular Affairs and Diplomatic Security of the Department of State on Roles, Responsibilities, and Collaboration at Visa Security Units Abroad*, January 11, 2011.

[73] For further discussion on the issues leading up to this MOU, see U.S. Government Accountability Office, *Border Security: DHS's Visa Security Program Needs to Improve Performance Evaluation and Better Address Visa Risk Worldwide*, GAO-11-315, March 31, 2011, http://www.gao.gov/products/GAO-11-315.

In: Immigration Visas
Editor: Donald Nowell

ISBN: 978-1-63321-970-0
© 2014 Nova Science Publishers, Inc.

Chapter 2

BORDER SECURITY: STATE COULD ENHANCE VISA FRAUD PREVENTION BY STRATEGICALLY USING RESOURCES AND TRAINING[*]

United States Government Accountability Office

WHY GAO DID THIS STUDY

Foreign nationals may apply for entry into the United States under dozens of different visa categories, depending on circumstances. State's Bureaus of Consular Affairs and Diplomatic Security share responsibility for the prevention of visa fraud, which is a serious problem that threatens the integrity of the process. Some applicants commit fraud to obtain travel documents through illegal means, such as using counterfeit identity documents or making false claims to an adjudicating officer. Visa fraud may facilitate illegal activities in the United States, including crimes of violence, human trafficking, and terrorism. This report examines (1) countries and visa categories that are subject to the most fraud; (2) State's use of technologies and resources to combat fraud; and (3) training requirements of State officials responsible for fraud prevention. GAO examined State's reports and data on fraud trends and

---

[*] This is an edited, reformatted and augmented version of the United States Government Accountability Office publication, GAO-12-888, dated September 2012.

statistics, examined resources and technologies to counter fraud, and observed visa operations and fraud prevention efforts overseas and domestically.

WHAT GAO RECOMMENDS

GAO recommends that State (1) formulate a policy to systematically utilize anti-fraud resources available at KCC, based on post workload and fraud trends, as determined by the Department and (2) establish requirements for FPM training in advanced anti-fraud technologies, taking advantage of distance learning technologies, and establishing methods to track the extent to which requirements are met. State concurred with these recommendations.

WHAT GAO FOUND

Certain countries and visa categories are subject to higher levels of fraud. In fiscal year 2010, almost 60 percent of confirmed fraud cases (9,200 out of 16,000) involved applicants from Brazil, China, Dominican Republic, India, and Mexico. Department of State (State) officials told GAO that fraud most commonly involves applicants for temporary visits to the United States who submit false documentation to overcome the presumption that they intend to illegally immigrate. Fraud is also perpetrated for immigrant visas and nonimmigrant visa categories such as temporary worker visas and student visas. In response to State efforts to combat visa fraud, unscrupulous visa applicants adapt their strategies, and as a result, fraud trends evolve over time.

State has a variety of technological tools and resources to assist consular officers in combating fraud, but does not have a policy for their systematic use. For example, State recently implemented fraud prevention technologies such as a fraud case management system that establishes connections among multiple visa applications, calling attention to potentially fraudulent activity. Overseas posts have Fraud Prevention Units that consist of a Fraud Prevention Manager (FPM) and locally employed staff who analyze individual fraud cases. In 2011, the ratio of Fraud Prevention Unit staff to fraud cases varied widely across overseas posts, causing disproportionate workloads. The Kentucky Consular Center (KCC) is a domestic resource available to posts that verifies information on certain visa applications. However, KCC services are only provided on an ad-hoc basis, and State does not have a policy for posts to systematically utilize its resources. For example, an FPM at a high fraud post told GAO that the post would like to utilize KCC anti-fraud services for screening certain visa categories, but did not know how to request KCC assistance.

Although State offers anti-fraud training courses at the Foreign Service Institute and online, it does not require FPMs to take them and does not track FPMs' enrollment. Consular officers receive limited fraud training as part of the initial consular course, and FPMs are not required to take advanced fraud training in new technologies. In addition, GAO found that 81 percent of FPM positions were filled by entry-level officers and 84 percent of FPM positions were designated as either part-time or rotational. Between October 2009 and July 2012, entry-level officers made up about 21 percent of the total students who registered for a course on detecting fraudulent documents, and State could not guarantee that FPMs were among them. Four out of the five FPMs with whom GAO spoke had not been trained in State's new fraud case management system.

Source: State.

Visa Applicants at a High Fraud Post Wait for Interviews with Consular Officials.

ABBREVIATIONS

ARSO-I	Assistant Regional Security Officer - Investigator
DHS	U.S. Department of Homeland Security
ECAS	Enterprise Case Assessment Service
ICE	Immigration and Customs Enforcement
KCC	Kentucky Consular Center
LES	Locally Employed Staff

MATRIX	Match Analytics and Trusted Real-time Identity X-Ref (or cross-reference)
MLB	Major League Baseball
RSO	Regional Security Officer
State	U.S. Department of State SWT Summer Work Travel
USCIS	U.S. Citizenship and Immigration Services

***

September 10, 2012

The Honorable Joseph I. Lieberman
Chairman
The Honorable Susan M. Collins
Ranking Member
Committee on Homeland Security and Governmental Affairs
United States Senate

The Department of State's (State) visa issuance process is the first line of defense against fraudulent or unlawful entry into the United States. State issues visas for both temporary visitors (referred to as nonimmigrant visas) and those seeking to enter the United States as permanent immigrants (referred to as immigrant visas). There are dozens of visa categories for entry, such as tourist visas, student visas, and temporary worker visas (see app. II for a list of all temporary visitor visa categories). State seeks to identify and prevent attempts by applicants to obtain travel documents through unauthorized means, such as knowingly altering or using counterfeit identity documents or intentionally making false claims or statements. Some applicants use fraudulently obtained visas to facilitate illegal activities in the United States, including crimes of violence, narcotics, human trafficking, and terrorism.

In 2005, we reported that State and other agencies had taken many steps to strengthen the visa process as an antiterrorism tool since the September 11, 2001 attacks. For example, State increased hiring of consular officers, revamped consular training with a focus on counterterrorism, and increased resources to combat visa fraud.[1] In 2007, we reported that the security of visas had been enhanced but more needed to be done to prevent their fraudulent use.[2] That same year, we reported that the Diversity Visa Program is particularly vulnerable to manipulation from an unscrupulous visa industry in some countries.[3]

This report examines (1) countries and visa categories subject to the most visa fraud; (2) State's technologies and resources to combat fraud; and (3) training requirements of State officials responsible for fraud prevention.

To determine the countries and visa categories subject to the most visa fraud, we analyzed State Fraud Digest reports from 1996 through 2012, reviewed fraud summaries for posts with high rates of fraud, reviewed compilations of Diplomatic Security Monthly Status reports, analyzed data on the number of visa applications referred to Fraud Prevention Units, and interviewed State officials at headquarters and abroad to discuss fraud trends. To assess State's use of technologies and resources to combat fraud, we met with State's Bureau of Consular Affairs Office of Consular Systems and Technology to review State's major data systems as well as the latest technological tools available to consular officers and Fraud Prevention Managers, and we visited the Kentucky Consular Center (KCC) to observe prescreening and anti-fraud activities. To understand the training required of State officials responsible for combating fraud, we gathered information about the training requirements of Fraud Prevention Managers and staff working in Fraud Prevention Units. We also analyzed data on the experience level of Fraud Prevention Managers at all 222 visa-issuing posts. Lastly, we conducted interviews with consular officials and Diplomatic Security Special Agents working in five overseas posts on issues related to visa fraud prevention.

We conducted our work from August 2011 through September 2012, in accordance with generally accepted government auditing standards. Those standards require that we plan and perform the audit to obtain sufficient, appropriate evidence to provide a reasonable basis for our findings and conclusions based on our audit objectives. We believe that the evidence obtained provides a reasonable basis for our findings and conclusions based on our audit objectives. (see appendix I for more information about our scope and methodology).

BACKGROUND

The mission of State's Bureau of Consular Affairs (Consular Affairs) is to protect the lives and interests of U.S. citizens overseas and to strengthen U.S. border security through the vigilant adjudication of U.S. passports and visas. Consular officers abroad have sole legal authority to adjudicate visa applications, and they receive overseas and domestic support to help identify visa fraud. Consular officers at overseas posts issue nonimmigrant visas to temporary visitors and immigrant visas to people who intend to immigrate to the United States.[4] The adjudication processes for both nonimmigrant and immigrant visa applications contain steps to check for fraud.

Consular Officers Rely on Overseas Support to Identify Fraud

Consular Affairs has more than 11,000 officers, local staff, and contractors working in over 300 locations around the world, including domestic visa centers and passport facilities. Within each consular section at overseas posts, consular officers adjudicate visa applications, serving as fraud detection officers on the first line of defense for border security. Consular officers are charged with facilitating legitimate travel while preventing ineligible aliens, including potential terrorists, from gaining admission to the United States. To help detect and prevent fraud, consular officers work with members of a Fraud Prevention Unit located in the consular section. In large posts, the Fraud Prevention Unit may be led by a Fraud Prevention Manager, and may be augmented at certain high-fraud posts by a Diplomatic Security Assistant Regional Security Officer Investigator.[5] In smaller posts, the Fraud Prevention Manager may be a consular officer who has other responsibilities depending on the workload volume and prevalence of fraud at the post. Consular officers may also coordinate with a Department of Homeland Security (DHS) Visa Security Officer and an external anti-fraud working group.

- *Fraud Prevention Manager.* Under the Bureau of Consular Affairs, fraud prevention efforts at the 222 visa-issuing posts are led by a Fraud Prevention Manager—a Foreign Service Officer assigned by consular management to investigate fraud cases, conduct fraud training, and provide information on fraud trends to the entire consular section. As of April 30, 2012, 81 percent of all visa issuing posts (180 of 222) had Fraud Prevention Manager positions filled by an entry-level officer or an officer of unspecified grade, and 84 percent of visa issuing posts (186 of 222) had Fraud Prevention Manager positions designated as part- time or rotational.[6] As of April 30, 2012, 36 posts had full-time mid-level Fraud Prevention Managers serving for 2 years. An additional 40 posts had full-time entry-level Fraud Prevention Managers serving for 2 years in positions originally designated for mid-level officers. Officers assigned to part-time Fraud

Prevention Manager positions have other consular-related duties in addition to preventing fraud. An officer filling the position on a rotational basis serves as the Fraud Prevention Manager for a designated period of time, typically 6 months, before moving on to other duties. State officials told us that the reason most Fraud Prevention Manager positions are part-time or rotational is in order to provide consular managers more flexibility in how they use consular staff, and also to provide officers with more opportunities to work on different activities.

- *Fraud Prevention Unit.* At 94 percent of visa-issuing posts (208 of 222), Fraud Prevention Managers have locally employed staff to assist them in fraud investigations, forming a Fraud Prevention Unit.[7] Out of the 3,700 locally employed staff working at consular posts, 417 are assigned to Fraud Prevention Units. These staff generally have special expertise in host country culture and language, as well as a network of local contacts to help develop leads on possible fraud. The Fraud Prevention Unit collects and verifies data for use in identifying fraud trends, analyzes individual fraud cases, and drafts and disseminates fraud reports. Tools utilized in individual fraud investigations vary from post to post, but may include physical document examination, visa record searches, facial-recognition review, phone calls to verify data, Internet searches, and site visits. Once all of the data have been collected, verified, and assessed, the Fraud Prevention Manager reviews the results and provides a final fraud finding to consular officers, who use the information to make a determination on whether to issue a visa to the applicant. If the Fraud Prevention Manager determines that the visa fraud may involve criminal activity, the case may be referred to Diplomatic Security agents at post for further investigation.
- Assistant Regional Security Officer Investigator. Under the Bureau of Diplomatic Security, 84 Assistant Regional Security Officer Investigators (ARSO-I) are assigned to 75 high-fraud posts to protect the integrity of the visa system and disrupt criminal networks and terrorist mobility.[8] ARSO-Is are Diplomatic Security Special Agents who specialize in criminal investigations of visa fraud.[9] Diplomatic Security recommends that ARSO-Is spend 80 percent of their time working on visa fraud, and 20 percent of their time supporting other Diplomatic Security responsibilities, such as providing security to high-level visitors at post. ARSO-Is often work with local law

enforcement and judicial officials to arrest and prosecute violators of local laws related to visa fraud, such as the fraudulent production of local identification documents used in applications for visas. Some investigations are connected to large-scale alien smuggling or human trafficking cases.

- DHS's U.S. Immigration and Customs Enforcement (ICE) Visa Security Program. ICE deploys Visa Security Officers to assist the consular section at designated high-risk posts by providing advice and training to consular officers regarding specific security threats, reviewing visa applications, and conducting investigations with respect to consular matters under the jurisdiction of the Secretary of Homeland Security.[10]
- External Anti-Fraud Working Group. At some posts, members of the Fraud Prevention Unit may coordinate with officials from other countries' embassies and consulates to share fraud trends in an anti-fraud working group.

Consular Officers Also Rely on Domestic Fraud Prevention Efforts

Domestically, both State and DHS play a role in fraud prevention and detection. While the Secretary of State has the lead role with respect to foreign policy-related visa issues, DHS is responsible for reviewing implementation of the policy and providing additional direction.

- State's Bureau of Consular Affairs Visa Office has direct responsibility for visa policy and oversight for the operations of KCC and the National Visa Center in New Hampshire.[11] These two centers prescreen visa applications for fraud and provide other support for visa adjudication worldwide.
- State's Bureau of Consular Affairs Office of Fraud Prevention Programs advises posts on visa and passport fraud questions, develops training material to manage fraud prevention programs, produces publications on fraud issues and trends, and coordinates with other U.S. agencies involved in preventing visa fraud.
- State's Diplomatic Security Office of Overseas Criminal Investigations Branch provides managerial oversight, guidance, and support to ARSO-Is at overseas posts.

- Diplomatic Security domestic field offices support overseas investigations by investigating visa fraud that is connected to criminal networks within the United States.
- DHS's U.S. Citizenship and Immigration Service (USCIS), Fraud Detection National Security Directorate is responsible for detecting, pursuing, and deterring immigration benefit fraud, and identifying persons seeking benefits who pose a threat to national security and public safety. In addition, Fraud Detection National Security Directorate staff conduct site visits and administrative inquiries within the United States on persons or entities suspected of immigration fraud and follow up with ICE investigators, law enforcement, and intelligence agencies on potential national security risks identified during background checks on immigration benefit applications.
- DHS's ICE Document and Benefit Fraud Task Forces work with federal, state, and local partners to detect, deter, investigate, and present instances of benefit fraud for criminal prosecution.
- DHS's Customs and Border Protection agents serve as the last line of defense in protecting American borders. Customs and Border Protection agents verify that visitors have proper travel documents and valid visas, and have the discretion to not admit travelers with valid visas into the United States if the agent suspects the traveler intends to violate the terms of his or her visa.

Issuance of Visas Has Generally Increased since 2003

After the September 11, 2001 terrorist attacks, the number of visas issued initially declined, but has generally increased steadily since 2003, and State anticipates demand for visas to continue to rise. As seen in figure 1, in 2001, the United States issued almost 8 million nonimmigrant and immigrant visas, based on data from the Consular Consolidated Database.[12] From 2001 to 2003, visa issuances declined by 34 percent. However, since then, the number of immigrant and nonimmigrant visas issued has generally trended upward. In 2011, consular officers issued more than 7.5 million nonimmigrant visas, up 54 percent from 2003 levels. Approximately 75 percent of the 7.5 million nonimmigrant visas issued in 2011 were processed for temporary visits to the United States for business or personal reasons, such as tourism.[13] More than half (52 percent) of the visas for temporary visits were issued to visitors from Brazil, China, India, and Mexico. According to the Deputy Assistant Secretary for Visa Services, State continues to see increases in visa demand for individuals residing in some of the world's fastest-growing economies.

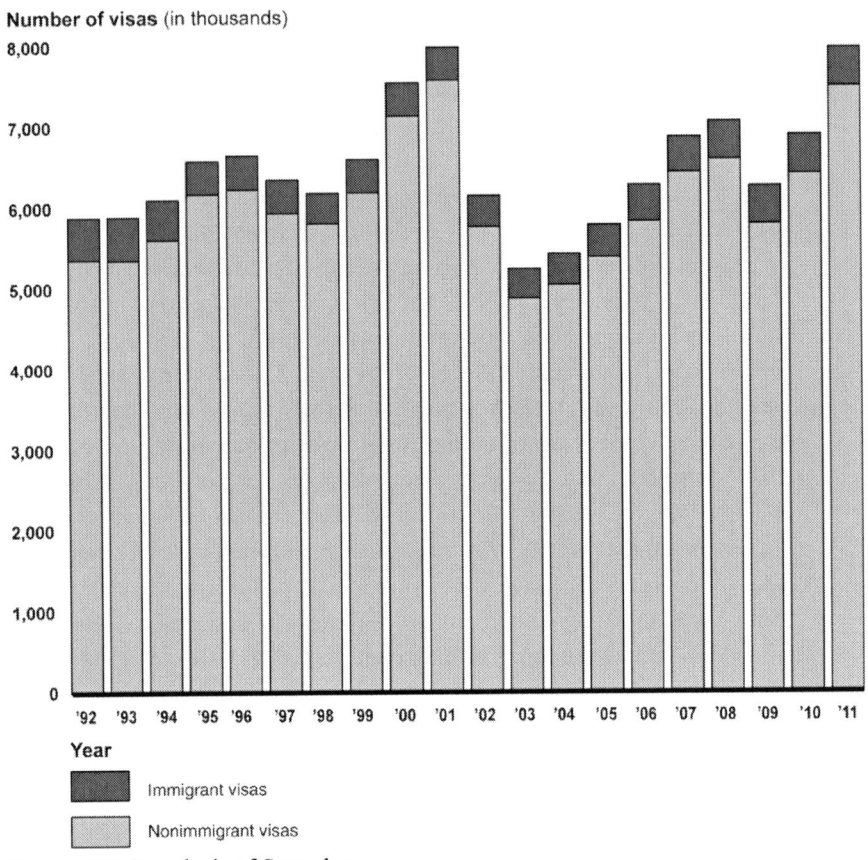

Source: GAO analysis of State data.

Figure 1. Nonimmigrant and Immigrant Visas Issued Worldwide, Fiscal Years 1992 to 2011.

While visa issuances have generally increased since 2003, visa refusals have fluctuated since 2006. In fiscal year 2011, more than 2.1 million nonimmigrant visa applicants worldwide were denied visas for entry into the United States.[14] As seen in table 1, adjusted refusal rates for tourist visas in Brazil, China, India, and Mexico fluctuated between fiscal years 2006 and 2011.[15] While refusals of visitors from Brazil, China, and Mexico have generally decreased in the last 6 years, refusals of visitors from India have increased. Visas may be refused for a number of reasons other than a suspicion of fraud, such as insufficient documentation or suspected immigration intent.[16] When a consular officer suspects that the applicant's travel or financial documents are counterfeit, the consular officer may deny the applicant's request for a visa or may refer the case to the Fraud Prevention Unit for an additional fraud assessment.[17]

The U.S. travel and tourism industry benefits from foreign visitors, and the U.S. government is working to accommodate an increase in demand for tourist travel. For example, State reported in 2010 that international tourists contributed $134 billion to the U.S. economy and supported over 1.1 million jobs. The Administration has encouraged State to increase visa processing capacity and reduce wait times for receiving a visa. In January 2012, President Obama issued an Executive Order requesting that the Secretaries of State and Homeland Security, in consultation with the Assistant to the President for Homeland Security and Counterterrorism and the Director of the Office of Management and Budget, develop an implementation plan to (1) increase nonimmigrant visa processing capacity in China and Brazil by 40 percent over the coming year and (2) ensure that 80 percent of nonimmigrant visa applicants are interviewed within 3 weeks of receipt of visa applications.

Table 1. Percentage of Tourist Visas Refused in Brazil, China, India, and Mexico, Fiscal Years 2006 to 2011

Country	2006	2007	2008	2009	2010	2011
Brazil	13	10	6	7	5	4
China	25	21	18	16	13	12
India	20	22	25	29	27	30
Mexico	31[a]	33[a]	11[a]	11[a]	11	13

Source: GAO analysis of State data in the Consular Consolidated Database.
[a] Does not include border crossing card applications.

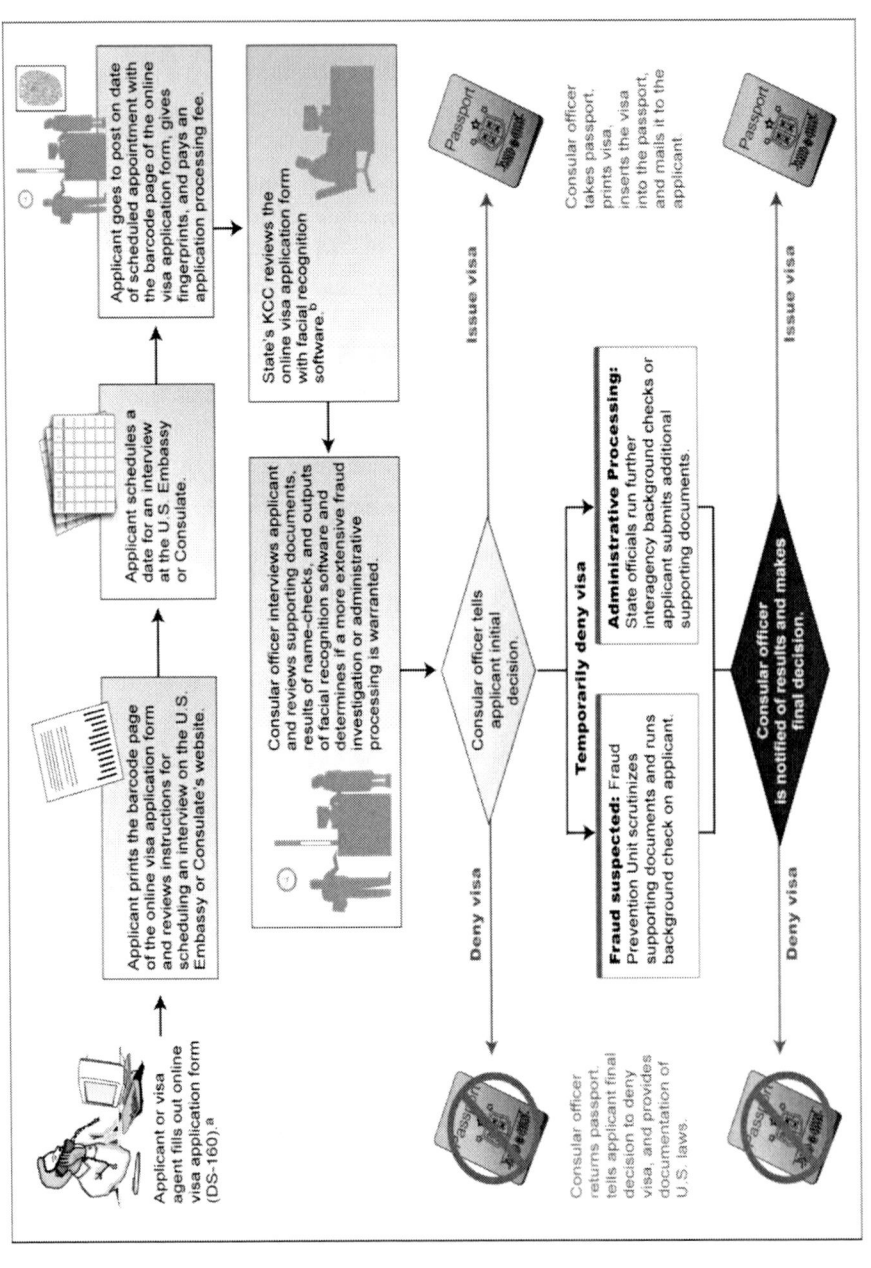

Source: GAO analysis of State data; Nova Development (clipart).

[a] Prior to this step, some nonimmigrant visas require petitioners to file a petition on behalf of the applicant with USCIS. USCIS is responsible for approving or denying the petition, notifying the petitioner, and sending the approved petition to KCC, where a file is created in the Petition Information Management System.

[b] KCC also prescreens work visas submitted to 24 high-fraud, high-volume posts based on information provided in the USCIS petition. Relevant information is entered into the comments on the DS-160 for consular officers to review at the time of the interview.

Figure 2. Standard Nonimmigrant Visa Adjudication Process at a U.S. Embassy or Consulate.

Nonimmigrant and Immigrant Visa Adjudication Processes Include Fraud Checks

Nonimmigrant Visa Adjudication Process

Almost all nonimmigrant visa applicants submit an online visa application called the DS-160 through State's web-based portal called the Consular Electronic Application Center, and then schedule a visa interview at a local U.S. embassy or consulate. Consular officers interview visa applicants, review the application and supporting documents, such as birth certificates, and make an initial decision to issue or deny the visa application. A consular officer may temporarily deny the visa in order to scrutinize the application for suspected fraud or to process it further administratively (see figure 2).

Immigrant Visa Adjudication Process

Obtaining an immigrant visa is one part of a four part process for aliens outside of the United States to become a permanent resident of the United States. First, an eligible U.S. citizen or lawful permanent resident, called a petitioner, must file a petition (a paper form) with USCIS on behalf of the alien applying for lawful permanent resident status, who is called the beneficiary. Generally, the petitioner can be either a relative[18] or employer, although there are visa categories in which the applicant can self petition, such as the diversity visa.[19] USCIS has the sole authority to approve or deny the petition. Second, once a petition is approved and a visa number is available in the appropriate category, the beneficiary prepares for a visa interview by gathering required documentation and undergoing a medical exam. Third, the beneficiary, now called the applicant, submits an online visa application, either the DS-260 or the DS-230, along with evidence supporting the applicant's eligibility, such as a birth certificate or diploma.[20] All aliens outside the United States apply for an immigrant visa at the U.S. consulate in their current country of residence. As in the nonimmigrant visa process, the alien schedules a visa interview, submits fingerprints, and pays a visa application processing fee. During the interview, a consular officer reviews submitted documentation as well as biometric and other security and fraud checks, determines if the alien is subject to any ineligibilities, and confirms that the applicant has the required legal relationship with the petitioner. The consular officer then either approves or denies the visa application. If the visa application is approved, a visa is printed and placed in the applicant's passport. Fourth, the applicant travels to the United States with his or her immigrant visa and packet of supporting documentation. Upon admission by a Customs and Border Patrol officer at the port of entry, the alien becomes a lawful permanent resident.

CERTAIN COUNTRIES AND VISA CATEGORIES EXPERIENCE HIGH LEVELS OF FRAUD, BUT TRENDS EVOLVE OVER TIME

Certain countries, such as Brazil, China, the Dominican Republic, India, and Mexico, had high numbers of suspected fraud cases in fiscal year 2010, and certain visa categories, such as work visas, student visas, and diversity visas, had high levels of fraud. Visa fraud has become more sophisticated over time with increased globalization, advanced technology, and ease of travel.

Although Fraud Conditions Are Post-Specific, Certain Countries Have High Numbers of Suspected Fraud Cases

State requires Fraud Prevention Managers to classify fraud levels at each post. Fraud Prevention Managers are required to submit a fraud assessment twice a year as part of the post's bi-annual fraud summary. Fraud assessments rank a post's fraud conditions as high, medium, or low, based on the ratio of visa applications referred to the Fraud Prevention Unit out of the total number of visa applications. The fraud assessment also includes the prevalence of corruption in the local environment, including the reliability of country documents and cooperation with local law enforcement. Additionally, ARSO-Is provide input into fraud assessments regarding the nature of criminal activity involving visas. According to State, a country with high numbers of suspected fraud cases may not necessarily be designated as a high-fraud country if its proportion of suspected fraud to visa applications is low.

Recently, State has taken steps to improve its ability to compare fraud levels across posts. In the past, according to State officials, self-reported fraud levels had not been used to assess posts' fraud conditions relative to other posts because posts had different methods for referring cases to Fraud Prevention Units.[21] Referrals to Fraud Prevention Units are considered an accurate portrayal of the volume of fraud cases handled at individual posts because Fraud Prevention Managers must make a fraud assessment for all cases that are referred. In July 2012, State distributed new guidance that clarifies when consular officers should refer visa applications to Fraud Prevention Units. For example, new guidance instructs consular officers to refer applications to Fraud Prevention Units whenever the unit is expected to expend resources to verify some aspect of an applicant's case or when consular officers cannot perform a needed task, such as verifying the employment of an applicant.

The volume of visas processed and the number of fraudulent applications vary from country to country. In general, fraudulent activity is found in a very small percentage of overall visas granted. Based on State's Consular Consolidated Database, 6.9 million nonimmigrant and immigrant visas were issued worldwide in 2010. That same year, approximately 74,000 visa applications were referred to Fraud Prevention Units for additional scrutiny. Of these, about 16,000, or 22 percent, were confirmed as fraudulent in fiscal year 2010.[22] Some countries may experience high visa demand but low numbers of suspected fraud cases, while other countries may experience high visa demand and high numbers of suspected fraud cases. For example, in 2010, consular officers throughout Brazil issued approximately 556,000 visas and referred about 3,000 visa applications to their Fraud Prevention Units, of which 750 (or 24 percent of visa applications suspected of fraud) were confirmed as fraudulent. Meanwhile, consular officers throughout India issued about 528,000 visas in 2010, referred about 5,200 visa applications to their Fraud Prevention Units, and confirmed about 2,600 (or 50 percent of visa applications suspected of fraud) as fraudulent. See figure 3 for the top 10 posts for referrals to Fraud Prevention Units among total nonimmigrant and immigrant visa applications in 2010. Almost 60 percent of confirmed fraud cases (9,200 out of 16,000) were referred to Fraud Prevention Units in Brazil, China, Dominican Republic, India, and Mexico in fiscal year 2010.[23]

Visa Fraud Concentrated in Nonimmigrant Visa Applications

State's Office of Fraud Prevention Programs reports that a majority of visa fraud involves nonimmigrant visa applicants who submit false documents or make false statements to obtain a tourist or business visitor visa. According to State officials, some visitor visa applicants provide fraudulent statements or documents, such as a false bank statement, to demonstrate strong ties with their home country and therefore overcome the presumption that they intend to use their temporary visitor visa to illegally immigrate to the United States. Denied visitor visa applications are not usually referred to the Fraud

Prevention Unit unless the officer suspects the case could be linked to organized crime.

Other kinds of fraud can be found in temporary worker visas, student visas, exchange visitor visas, immigrant visas, and diversity visas.

- *Temporary Worker Visas*: While State officials said that most work visas facilitate legitimate travel, fraud has been found among petitioners and applicants for both skilled worker and temporary agricultural worker visas.[24] Some petitioners in the United States create phony companies and petition for workers to join them in the United States, usually with the applicants' knowledge and participation in the fraudulent activity, according to State officials. Other examples of fraud include cases in which educational degrees were found to be fraudulent, signatures were forged on supporting documents, and workers performed duties or received payments significantly different from those described in the applications. A recent DHS study reported that 21 percent of skilled worker petitions they examined involved fraud or technical violations.[25] In 2005, DHS began collecting an additional $500 fee on certain work visas to be used for fraud prevention and detection purposes.[26]
- *Student Visas*: Foreign students interested in studying in the United States must first be admitted to a school or university before applying for a visa at a U.S. embassy or consulate overseas.[27] The process for determining who will be issued or refused a visa contains several steps, including documentation reviews, in-person interviews, collection of applicants' fingerprints, and cross-references against multiple databases of information.[28] In 2011, State issued over 486,000 student visas, of which 71 percent were issued to students from Asia. According to the Fraud Prevention Coordinator for India, fraud among student visa applications is common throughout India. For example, some exam centers that offer the Test of English as a Foreign Language (TOEFL) are suspected of being complacent when students cheat on the exam in order to achieve high scores. If a student applicant cannot answer a consular officer's questions in English, yet received 105 out of 120 on their TOEFL score, fraud may be present, according to a consular officer in New Delhi.

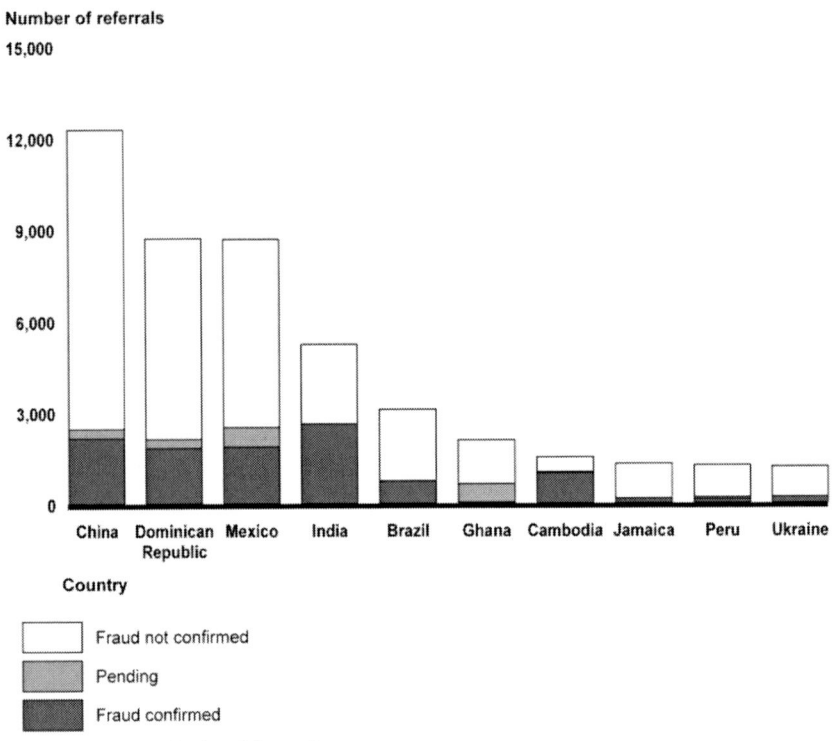

Source: GAO analysis of State data.

Figure 3. Top 10 Countries for Referrals to Fraud Prevention Units, Fiscal Year 2010.

- *Exchange Visitor Visas*: Summer Work and Travel (SWT) visas are a subset of the Exchange Visitor Program, and are susceptible to fraud.[29] The Exchange Visitor Program fosters global understanding through educational and cultural exchanges. All exchange visitors are expected to return to their home country upon completion of their program in order to share their experiences. In 2011, 35 percent (108,717) of the total exchange visitors (306,429) were granted entry into the United States for the purpose of "Summer Work and Travel." According to State officials, many SWT visa applicants misrepresent their status as students or their intentions for using the SWT visa. Additionally, many U.S. sponsors falsely represent their businesses and how they intend to employ SWT applicants. U.S. sponsors have been found to exploit SWT visa holders for financial gain. On May 10, 2012, State's Bureau of Education and Cultural Exchange issued rules that are expected to protect the health, safety, and welfare of

- SWT program participants. The rules provide a cap on the number of annual SWT program participants that may be granted visas.[30]
- *Immigrant Visas*: In 2010, State issued 482,052 immigrant visas. That same year, 21,013 immigrant visa applications were referred to Fraud Prevention Units and 4,984 (or about 24 percent) were confirmed as fraudulent. Immigrant visa fraud can take many forms. At several posts we visited, State officials said a common problem involved applicants who pay American citizens to marry them or who falsely represent their intentions to citizens and deceive them into marriage in order to obtain lawful permanent residence in the United States. In a typical immigrant visa fraud case, an individual divorces his or her spouse in a foreign country, marries an American citizen, and, after living in the United States for a certain period of time, obtains U.S. citizenship or legal permanent resident status, divorces the U.S. spouse, and remarries the original spouse so that they can reunite in the United States.
- *Diversity Visas*: The Diversity Visa Program was established through the Immigration Act of 1990 and provides up to 55,000 immigrant visas annually to aliens from countries with low rates of immigration to the United States.[31] Aliens register for the diversity visa lottery for free online and applicants are randomly selected for interviews through a lottery process. Upon being selected, a winner must apply for a visa, be interviewed, and be found eligible for the diversity visa. All countries are eligible for the Diversity Visa Program except those from which more than 50,000 immigrants have come to the United States over the preceding 5 years. In 2011, approximately 16.5 million people applied for the program and about 107,000 (7 percent) were selected for further processing. Of those selected, 75,000 were interviewed at posts for a diversity visa, and approximately 50,000 received visas. Because the program does not require a U.S.-based petitioner, it is particularly susceptible to fraud. Diversity visa fraud is rampant in parts of South Asia, Africa, and Eastern Europe, and is particularly acute in areas where few individuals have independent access to the Internet.[32] A typical scenario includes visa facilitators, travel agents, or Internet café operators who help would-be applicants submit an entry for a fee. Many of these facilitators withhold the confirmation information that the entrant must use to retrieve his or her selection status. To access the lottery notification, the facilitators may require winning applicants to either pay an additional exorbitant

fee or agree to enter into a marriage with another of the facilitator's paying clients solely for the purpose of extending immigration benefits.

Fraud Risks Evolve over Time

Visa fraud has evolved and become more sophisticated over time due to unscrupulous visa applicants who adapt to State's efforts to combat fraud, increased globalization, advanced technology, and ease of travel. Fraud schemes are no longer centralized in individual countries. Criminal fraud rings, human smuggling networks, and trafficking rings work across multiple countries to circumvent State's visa process. For example, in 2009, a typical route for traffickers from India who sought religious asylum in the United States originated in New Delhi and transited through Moscow, Dubai, Sao Paulo, and Mexico before reaching Texas, according to the Assistant Regional Security Officer Investigator in New Delhi. In addition, new technologies have helped individuals and organizations adapt to State's visa security features and develop increasingly sophisticated fraud schemes. For example, high-quality micro-printing and new assembly methods have allowed imposters to duplicate State's visa security threads and serial numbers. With global access to the Internet, fraud scams used in one country or continent have quickly made their way to others, and therefore high-fraud countries and posts have shifted from year to year. For example, only 4 countries were among the top 10 countries for visa fraud in both 2005 and 2010: the Dominican Republic, Ghana, Jamaica, and Peru.[33]

STATE HAS A VARIETY OF TOOLS AND RESOURCES TO COMBAT FRAUD, BUT DOES NOT HAVE A POLICY FOR SYSTEMATICALLY UTILIZING DOMESTIC ANTI-FRAUD RESOURCES

Consular officers rely on State's advanced information technology, fraud reports, and domestic and overseas fraud prevention resources to improve their ability to detect and deter fraud. However, State does not have a policy to systematically utilize its domestic anti-fraud resources to offset fraud workload overseas.

State Has Implemented New Technological Tools Intended to Enhance Its Visa Fraud Prevention Efforts

The Consular Affairs Office of Consular Systems and Technology has deployed several new tools to counter fraud in the visa process, including the following:

- *Online Nonimmigrant Visa Application Form, DS-160*: In the spring of 2010, State implemented the DS-160 online nonimmigrant visa application system, which requires applicants to submit all information electronically. With the collection of electronic information prior to the scheduled visa interview, State is able to research and analyze applicants' data for indicators of fraud prior to an interview with a consular officer. Overseas, State encourages Fraud Prevention Units to conduct pre-screening checks of applicants' visa history to identify aliases or discrepancies between current and previous applications.
- *Enterprise Case Assessment Service (eCAS)*: In April 2011, State released eCAS, the first centralized system for Fraud Prevention Units to track and manage their nonimmigrant and immigrant visa fraud cases. eCAS is based in the Consular Consolidated Database, and Fraud Prevention Units use it to create, develop, and resolve fraud assessments. Previously, fraud cases were either designated as "fraud confirmed" or "fraud not confirmed." With eCAS, fraud cases are now designated as "fraud confirmed," "no fraud," or "inconclusive," which allows Fraud Prevention units more flexibility to designate that some cases have a suspicion of fraud but not enough evidence to confirm fraud. In the first 5 months of the system's use, May 2011 through September 2011, 188 posts worldwide used eCAS to process over 43,000 fraud cases. According to State, in 2012 State released an eCAS module domestically that can also be used to process passport fraud cases, and State plans to extend this module overseas in 2013.
- *MATRIX*: In 2011, State released a new fraud prevention tool known as MATRIX that is accessible to Fraud Prevention Units and Diplomatic Security agents through State's Consular Consolidated Database.[34] MATRIX is a search tool that makes associations between information on a visa application and other records and data sources. MATRIX links information in the Consular Consolidated Database to other State records, USCIS records, and INTERPOL data.[35] Fraud

Prevention Managers and ARSO-Is can use MATRIX to link information contained on previous visa applications and to reveal similarities across multiple applications as an indicator of fraud. For example, according to Consular Affairs officials, MATRIX found that one applicant's contact phone number in the United States matched the phone numbers used by 17 other applicants, a possible indication of fraud.

- *Diversity Visa Entry Status Check*: In 2010, State began an online verification system called the Entry Status Check that allowed all entrants of the 2010 Diversity Visa Program to electronically, individually, and privately check the status of their online submissions through a State website. This system eliminated the need for direct mailing of Diversity Visa correspondence and enhanced State's ability to combat fraud. Prior to the electronic system, notification letters were physically mailed to the address listed on the application. Unscrupulous visa agents listed their own addresses so that the notification letters were delivered to them instead of the people selected in the lottery. The agent could demand thousands of dollars from an applicant in exchange for the letter.
- *Consular Consolidated Database Search Rules to Identify Fraud Indicators*: State is currently developing a new anti-fraud tool that will automatically search visa applications for fraud indicators and alert consular officials when fraud indicators are found. For example, State may find higher rates of fraud among visa applicants who rely on services provided by a particular local visa company. Consular officials in that country can request that State flag future visa applications listing that visa company's name.

State Compiles Various Internal Reports to Share Information about Fraud Trends and Available Resources

State shares information between consular posts and headquarters regarding the latest fraud trends through reporting mechanisms such as validation studies, semi-annual fraud summaries, fraud digests, fraud notices, or reporting cables, Diplomatic Security monthly status reports, and Diplomatic Security program reviews.

Border Security 49

- *Validation Studies*: State considers validation studies to be one of the best fraud-prevention tools available to consular officers. Posts conduct validation studies on visas that have been issued to determine the extent to which the visas have been misused, and posts send summaries of fraud risks to headquarters twice a year. Posts are required to conduct at least two validation studies per year, one on a visa category of the post's choosing and one on visa referrals.[36] Generally, consular officers select a sample of visa issuances and determine how many of the visa recipients departed the United States within the terms of their visas, how many remained in the United States longer than their visas allowed, and how many never traveled to the United States.[37] Validation studies help measure the accuracy of adjudication decisions, and allow Consular Affairs officials to share emerging fraud trends across posts.
- *Semi-Annual Fraud Summaries*: State guidance calls for validation studies to be incorporated into posts' Semi-Annual Fraud Summaries—reports submitted twice annually that provide input for improvements in fraud prevention guidance, training, and resources. State guidance notes that the summaries should discuss current country conditions that may contribute to fraud risks, such as the presence of organized crime networks. According to the guidance, the summaries should discuss fraud trends for nonimmigrant visas, immigrant visas, diversity visas, passports, and coordination with Diplomatic Security personnel, among other topics. These studies should discuss new information that may be used to establish new fraud indicators.
- *Fraud Digests*: Since September 1996, State has published a monthly newsletter called the Fraud Digest that profiles worldwide fraud trends, fraud prevention techniques, and advances in areas such as fraud prevention technology and immigration document design. The digests are accessible on the web and are shared government-wide with approximately 3,600 subscribers, as of April 2012. The main audience for the digest is domestic and overseas consular personnel and Diplomatic Security agents.
- *Reporting Cables*: State headquarters gathers and analyzes information from posts, and distributes guidance to posts through monthly reporting cables in order to update consular officers on evolving fraud trends.

- *Diplomatic Security Monthly Status Reports*: According to Diplomatic Security officials, ARSO-Is worldwide submit monthly status reports that delineate the number of hours spent on criminal investigations and training of foreign personnel. The status report also describes progress on the post's visa cases, including preliminary queries for information and arrests. The information supplements data entered into the Diplomatic Security primary case management system known as the Investigative Management System, according to Diplomatic Security officials.
- *Diplomatic Security Program Reviews*: Diplomatic Security officials told us that Diplomatic Security program reviews are internal reports that highlight best practices at posts and make recommendations for improvements. To complete the program reviews, officials from Diplomatic Security's Office of Criminal Investigations told us that they spend 2 days at each post answering standardized questions about training, pending cases, arrests, budget, and information systems, among other topics. Diplomatic Security aims to visit all posts with an ARSO-I presence once every 2 years, according to Diplomatic Security officials.

State Has Expanded Anti-Fraud Activities Conducted by KCC

KCC, located in Williamsburg, Kentucky, has become an important anti-fraud resource for State. State opened KCC in October 2000, to process worldwide diversity visa applications and reduce the workload on adjudicating officers at overseas posts. According to KCC officials, the number of local employees at KCC has increased from 40 to 273, including 54 staff working within a Fraud Prevention Unit.[38] In August 2001, KCC began a pilot project to screen all nonimmigrant visa applications with facial recognition software. According to KCC officials, after the September 11, 2001 attack, State was required to store visa applications for 7 years. As a result, KCC officials began scanning old visa applications and uploading all biographic information and evidence of visa ineligibilities. All visa applicants' biographic information, including both fingerprints and digitized photographs, is checked through State's Consular Lookout and Support System database and facial recognition software.

Border Security 51

Workers at the Kentucky Consular Center support Overseas Visa Adjudication

Source: State.

State describes KCC as an incubator for new consular projects, and KCC is in the process of expanding anti-fraud services to posts overseas, according to KCC officials. Currently, KCC provides prescreening services for selected posts overseas. Any post may request KCC assistance in conducting research and analysis on visa applications, either on an ad-hoc basis for individual cases, or on a pilot basis for larger-scale projects. For example, since over 50 percent of all skilled worker (H-1B) and intracompany transfers (L) visas are processed in India, KCC initiated a process to verify all petitioner information contained on these types of visa applications from posts in India, according to State officials. Globally, KCC screened 81,862 H-1B and L-1 applications for fraud in calendar year 2011. In addition to H and L visas, KCC conducts prescreening on several other visa classifications that are susceptible to fraud. According to State officials, KCC screeners and fraud analysts conduct basic checks, such as verifying the legal name of the business as well as more complex research including data mining, evaluation of the petitioning organization's business viability, and phone calls to petitioning employers. Additionally, KCC fraud analysts may also refer the case to onsite Fraud Detection and National Security officers to request a visit to the proposed employment site. If derogatory information, such as a revocation of a prior petition, exists on a petitioning company, screeners enter all comments into the applicant's online DS-160 form, for access by the consular officer, who makes the ultimate decision to issue or deny the visa.

In fiscal year 2012, State intends to prescreen 15 percent of all worldwide nonimmigrant and immigrant visa applications prior to the visa interview, increasing to 50 percent by fiscal year 2013. To prescreen visa applications, KCC reviews and processes all sets of documents and data received from petitioners and beneficiaries. KCC employees conduct research on visa applicants and petitioners, and provide this information to consular officers overseas so that they have access to the information prior to interviewing a visa applicant in person.[39] For example, we observed a KCC analyst conducting research on a summer work and travel visa application that listed the sponsor business as a restaurant. However, the KCC analyst determined that the physical address listed on the visa application was an adult entertainment venue, a business prohibited by the program. The KCC analyst notified the interviewing post of this finding so that the adjudicating officer would have knowledge of it before the interview. KCC now prescreens the vast majority of certain visa categories that have been associated with high rates of fraud, such as summer work and travel visas. From March 2011 to April 2012, KCC analysts researched over 9,000 companies participating in the Summer Work and Travel Program and found that 13 percent of them had fraud indicators. For example, some companies did not exist, the company's phone number was invalid, or the company reported that it never expected a summer work and travel participant.

Overseas Anti-Fraud Staffing Levels and Workload Vary by Post

Anti-fraud staffing levels in Fraud Prevention Units vary widely across overseas posts, causing disproportionate workloads. State assigns personnel to Fraud Prevention Units based on input from post management and consular affairs management at headquarters. Personnel from State's Office of Fraud Prevention Programs said resource decisions for Fraud Prevention Units are driven by visa workload and other factors at posts, not by the number of fraud cases.[40] Although statistics on the number of fraud cases confirmed, unconfirmed, or inconclusive are used by posts to direct anti-fraud strategies, Consular Affairs does not use these statistics to determine the appropriate distribution of personnel to Fraud Prevention Units.

The posts with the highest numbers of suspected fraud cases in 2011 were not assigned a number of Fraud Prevention Unit staff proportionate to the number of fraud cases, as seen in table 2. For example, one entry level officer and one mid-level officer in Santo Domingo, who were assigned to Fraud Prevention Manager positions, joined five locally employed staff in the Embassy's Fraud Prevention Unit to combat the entire country's visa fraud. With approximately 7,879 cases suspected of fraud in 2011, each member of Santo Domingo's Fraud Prevention Unit investigated an average of 1,126 cases and each member of Guangzhou's Fraud Prevention Unit investigated an average of 239 cases that year.

State Does Not Have a Policy for Utilizing Domestic Anti-Fraud Resources to Offset Posts' Fraud Workload

According to State officials, while State plans to expand the use of KCC anti-fraud resources, there is no systematic process for overseas posts to formally request KCC prescreening assistance. State's Program Evaluation Policy notes that program evaluation is essential for planning decisions, and evaluation findings should be integrated into program strategies and policies. However, State officials told us that anti-fraud pilot programs conducted at KCC are not formally evaluated and there is no established policy for posts to access domestic anti-fraud resources.[41] Rather, KCC provides anti-fraud assistance to overseas posts on an ad-hoc basis based on informal communication.[42]

According to KCC's Director, most posts have not requested KCC's assistance because they are not familiar with all of the anti-fraud services that KCC can provide or how to request services. For example, a Fraud Prevention Manager in a high-fraud post that we visited told us that the post would like additional KCC prescreening of certain visa categories, but was unaware of how to request KCC assistance. Multiple State officials told us that most KCC prescreening initiatives have been due to institutional knowledge at the management level in the field. For example, all India-specific services provided by KCC were a direct result of a Consular Manager in India who was aware of the prescreening services KCC could provide.

According to the KCC Director, there are clear benefits to utilizing KCC for fraud investigations. KCC staff are fully vetted U.S. citizens with secret clearances and access to all restricted databases used in visa adjudications. In addition, both Diplomatic Security and the U.S. Citizenship and Immigration Service are represented at KCC, and are available to assist in fraud investigations. The majority of KCC staff are provided through a contractor, and the contract provides for the ability to adjust to changes in demand for services.

Table 2. Type and Number of Staff Assigned to Fraud Prevention Units and Ratio of Staff to Suspected Fraud Cases, Fiscal Year 2011

Posts with highest numbers of suspected fraud cases in 2011	Level and number of Fraud Prevention Managers	Number of locally employed staff	Total Fraud Prevention Unit staff[a]	Number of suspected fraud cases[b]	Ratio of Fraud Prevention Unit staff to cases
Santo Domingo, the Dominican Republic	1 mid-level officer, 1 entry-level officer	5	7	7879	1:1126
Kyiv, Ukraine	1 mid-level officer	7	8	7675	1:959
Ciudad Juarez, Mexico	1 mid-level officer, 1 part-time or rotational officer	11	13	3620	1:278
Shanghai, China	1 mid-level officer, 2 entry-level officers	5	8	3068	1:384
Beijing, China	1 mid-level officer, 2 part-time or rotational officers	3	6	3047	1:508
Posts with highest numbers of suspected fraud cases in 2011	Level and number of Fraud Prevention Managers	Number of locally employed staff	Total Fraud Prevention Unit staff[a]	Number of suspected fraud cases[b]	Ratio of Fraud Prevention Unit staff to cases
Guangzhou, China	1 mid-level officer, 2 entry-level officers	7	10	2386	1:239
Shenyang, China	1 mid-level officer, 1 part-time officer	5	7	2350	1:336
Bogota, Colombia	1 mid-level officer, 2 entry-level officers	4	7	2293	1:328
Accra, Ghana	1 mid-level officer	3	4	1726	1:432
New Delhi, India	1 mid-level officer, 1 entry-level officer	6	8	1640	1:205

Source: GAO analysis of State data.

a Staffing data was gathered as of April 30, 2012.

b The suspected number of fraud cases is based on data from eCAS for the period of May 1, 2001 through September 30, 2011, as well as data from State's previous fraud tracking system for the period of October 1, 2010 through April 30, 2011.

ALTHOUGH STATE OFFERS A VARIETY OF ANTI-FRAUD TRAINING COURSES, FRAUD PREVENTION MANAGERS ARE NOT REQUIRED TO TAKE THEM

Although State offers anti-fraud courses in a classroom setting and online, State does not require Fraud Prevention Managers to take them. In addition, State does not track Fraud Prevention Manager enrollment in anti-fraud courses, and therefore State does not know whether the large number of entry-level officers filling fraud prevention manager positions have taken the anti-fraud courses.

State Offers a Variety of Anti-Fraud Training Courses

The Foreign Service Institute has expanded the number of courses it offers Foreign Service Officers in fraud prevention and detection, covering topics such as advanced name checking, analytic interviewing, and emotional content analysis.[43] The institute's anti-fraud training courses include the following:

- *Basic Consular Course (PC530)*: Commonly known as ConGen, PC530 is a 6-week course that all Foreign Service officers are required to take prior to their first consular tour. PC530 is also required for any officer heading to a consular tour who has neither done consular work nor taken ConGen in the preceding 5 years. The course contains a module covering security, accountability, fraud, and ethics, which includes training in detecting and preventing fraud.
- *Fraud Prevention for Consular Managers (PC541)*: This course is designed for Fraud Prevention Managers who are currently serving in the field, emphasizing anti-fraud and counterterrorism tools for consular officers.[44]

State also offers consular officers distance learning or online courses in detecting and preventing fraud. These courses are either prescheduled live courses, prerecorded or accessible 24 hours a day, or offered on-demand. Online consular training in fraud includes the following:

- *Detecting Imposters (PC128)*: This course teaches students procedures for identifying imposters either at the interview window or in photographs.
- *Detecting Fraudulent Documents (PC544)*: This course teaches consular officers how to determine whether a document has been altered or is counterfeit.
- *New Consular Technologies (eCAS and MATRIX)*: This course trains consular officers in how to use eCAS and MATRIX to combat visa fraud.

State officials from the Office of Consular Systems and Technology said that its training programs are updated as soon as new features are rolled out, and the training typically focuses on new technology features. Consular officers are provided with manuals that explain the new software tools about a month in advance and can attend live and prerecorded training courses. While some consular courses can take about 2 hours, training in MATRIX is a prerecorded session that takes approximately 30 minutes. Although training on new technological tools is available and encouraged by State, a survey of Fraud Prevention Managers revealed that respondents' lack of knowledge of some key anti-fraud tools indicated that updates were not uniformly reaching officers.[45]

State Does Not Require Fraud Prevention Managers to Take Anti-Fraud Courses

While State encourages Fraud Prevention Managers to take updated fraud prevention training, the training is not required. Entry-level officers are required to complete 6 weeks of basic consular training prior to their arrival at post but are not required to take other advanced anti-fraud courses offered at the Foreign Service Institute or online, such as eCAS or MATRIX. For example, four of the five Fraud Prevention Managers we met with had not been trained in MATRIX. Advanced fraud training courses are targeted to mid-level officers, but the majority of Fraud Prevention Manager positions

(180 of 222) were filled by an entry-level officer or an officer of unspecified grade. In 2011, a little more than half of the students enrolled in PC541 were entry-level officers, and State could not determine whether Fraud Prevention Managers were among them. Additionally, between October 2009 and July 2012, entry-level officers made up approximately 22 percent (489 of 2,252) of the total number of students who registered for Detecting Imposters (PC128) and 21 percent (486 of 2,246) of the total number of students who registered for Detecting Fraudulent Documents (PC544). Without advanced fraud training courses, Fraud Prevention Managers may not know about the roles and responsibilities of KCC, or how to use the Consular Lookout and Support System name-check database and biometric systems. For example, two of the five Fraud Prevention Managers with whom we met were unfamiliar with the anti-fraud services available at KCC. According to the Office of Fraud Prevention Program's country desk officers, the level of anti-fraud training offered to Foreign Service Officers largely depends on the officer's experience level, years in the Foreign Service, and available time. Desk officers offer a 1-hour briefing of country-specific fraud issues and resources to all Foreign Service Officers prior to their deployment, but not all of the officers take advantage of the briefing, according to officials from the Office of Fraud Prevention Programs.

In addition, a significant period of time may pass between an entry-level officer's completion of the basic consular course and the time when he or she assumes the role of Fraud Prevention Manager. Entry-level officers are required to take only limited fraud prevention training that does not include new anti-fraud technologies. For example, officers may not arrive at a post until they complete required language training, which can take 6 months to a year. Additionally, entry-level officers who are not on the consular affairs career track may serve a rotation in a different specialty area before serving a rotation in consular affairs. Finally, many entry-level officers are not assigned to the Fraud Prevention Manager position until after they arrive at post.

State Does Not Track Enrollment of Fraud Prevention Managers in Anti-Fraud Courses

While State offers these anti-fraud training courses, both in Washington D.C., and online, it does not track whether Fraud Prevention Managers are taking them. In 2012, four of the five Fraud Prevention Managers with whom we met had not been formally trained in MATRIX.[46] Since its rollout, State has not tracked the number of Fraud Prevention Managers that have been trained in eCAS and MATRIX. In addition, State was unable to differentiate enrollment data by position and therefore could not confirm that Fraud Prevention Managers had enrolled in any fraud prevention course.

CONCLUSION

State's fraud prevention efforts protect the integrity of the visa process and help prevent people from exploiting the visa process to commit crimes or threaten the security of the United States. Fraud trends evolve over time as criminal networks and unscrupulous visa applicants seek to circumvent State's visa application process. Meanwhile, the number of visas issued has risen steadily since 2003 and consular officers face increased pressure to expedite visa processing. The evolving nature of fraud and increases in the volume of visas adjudicated require State to continuously update its anti-fraud efforts. In recent years, State has taken steps to enhance the tools and services available to combat visa fraud, including the deployment of new anti-fraud technologies and resources improving State's ability to prescreen applications for indicators of fraud and to readily access information from prior visa applications. However, these technologies and resources are only useful if consular officers know that they exist and know how to use them. Currently, the majority of Fraud Prevention Manager positions are filled by entry-level officers, who are not the targeted audience for advanced anti-fraud training, and State does not require them to be trained in all anti-fraud technologies. As a result, Fraud Prevention Managers may not be fully equipped to detect and combat fraud. Furthermore, posts increasingly rely on KCC to prescreen certain visa applications for fraud, and State intends to prescreen 50 percent of all visa applications worldwide prior to consular interviews. However, State does not have a policy that specifies how to systematically utilize the center's resources, based on post workload and fraud trends. Therefore, State cannot be assured that a valuable tool to combat fraud is being strategically utilized. Absent effective support and training, Fraud Prevention Units may make uninformed decisions, thus enabling ineligible aliens, including potential terrorists, to gain admission to the United States.

RECOMMENDATIONS

To further improve the visa fraud prevention process, we recommend that the Secretary of State take the following two actions:

(1) Formulate a policy to systematically utilize anti-fraud resources available at the Kentucky Consular Center, based on post workload and fraud trends, as determined by the department; and
(2) Establish standardized training requirements for Fraud Prevention Managers, to include training in advanced anti-fraud technologies, taking advantage of distance learning technologies, and establishing methods to track the extent to which requirements are met.

AGENCY COMMENTS

We provided a draft of our report to State and DHS. State and DHS provided technical comments, which we incorporated as appropriate. State also provided written comments. State concurred with our recommendations.

Michael J. Courts,
Acting Director, International Affairs and Trade

APPENDIX I. SCOPE AND METHODOLOGY

This report examines (1) countries and visa categories subject to the most visa fraud; (2) technologies and resources to combat fraud; and (3) training requirements of State officials responsible for fraud prevention. This report focuses on visa fraud, and not passport fraud.[47]

To determine the countries and visa categories subject to the most visa fraud, and the evolution of fraud over time, we reviewed nonimmigrant and immigrant visa issuance data from the Consular Consolidated Database from 1992 to 2011. While we did not analyze State data on the number of visa applications during this time period, we reviewed visa refusal percentages by country. We did not review the reliability of these data because they were for background purposes only. We also reviewed State Fraud Digest reports from September 1996 through May 2012, semi-annual fraud summaries for some of the posts with the highest numbers of suspected fraud cases, and Diplomatic Security Monthly Status reports from fiscal year 2011. We also analyzed fiscal year 2010 and 2011 data on the number of visa applications referred to Fraud Prevention Units. We found 2010 data more reliable because State transitioned to a new fraud management system in the middle of fiscal year 2011, and formal guidance on how and when to refer cases to Fraud Prevention Units was not released until July 2012. We compared the 2005 Country Fraud Ranking of Posts to fiscal year 2010 data on the countries with the highest numbers of suspected fraud cases. We found these data to be sufficiently reliable for the purposes of indicating the countries that reported the highest volumes of reported fraud cases and made the most referrals. However, we found that these data may not accurately reflect the relative levels of actual fraud in each country due to possible differences in reporting by posts. We used fiscal year 2010 data for our analysis because State introduced a new data system in 2011, and we noted some potential problems with the 2011 data that arose due to the transition. State officials in the Office of Fraud Prevention Programs provided qualitative information on the types of visa categories that are subject to fraud. Lastly, we interviewed State officials at headquarters and abroad to discuss recent fraud trends.

To assess State's use of technologies and resources to combat fraud, we met with State's Bureau of Consular Affairs Office of Consular Systems and Technology to review State's major data systems as well as the latest technological tools available to consular officers and Fraud Prevention Managers. Specifically, we received demonstrations on State's newly deployed Enterprise Case Assessment Service (eCAS) used for tracking fraud cases, and MATRIX, a search tool used in fraud prevention. We visited the Kentucky Consular Center, an anti-fraud resource available to posts, and observed its activities. We interviewed State officials at posts regarding their usage of these tools and resources. To determine the reliability of data captured by eCAS on the number of cases referred to Fraud Prevention Units and the number of confirmed cases, we met with consular officers and Fraud Prevention Managers in five posts to determine how information was entered into eCAS. We determined that the eCAS system was widely used across posts and was sufficiently reliable to determine the general volume of fraud referrals.

To understand the training required of State officials responsible for combating fraud, we gathered information about training requirements and course enrollment from the Foreign Service Institute's Student Training Management System. We interviewed Foreign Service Institute personnel regarding controls, strengths and limitations of the course enrollment data and determined it was sufficiently reliable for our purposes. We also analyzed data on the number of direct hire and local staff working in all 222 visa-issuing consular posts as of December 2011 and reviewed data gathered by State liaisons from the Consular Workload Statistics System on the number and grade of officers assigned to Fraud Prevention Units at consular posts as of April 2012. We obtained staffing data from State's GEMS database. We tested the data on direct hires and local staff working at visa-issuing posts for completeness, confirmed the general accuracy of the data with select overseas posts, and interviewed knowledgeable officials from the Office of Resource Management and Organizational Analysis concerning the reliability of the data. We assessed data on the number and grade of officers assigned to Fraud Prevention Units for reliability, and interviewed Consular Affairs officials regarding how the data was collected and entered into the database, the controls and reviews of the data collection, and the major strengths and limitations of the data. We found the data to be sufficiently reliable for our purposes. Lastly, we conducted interviews with visa chiefs, Fraud Prevention Managers, and DS Assistant Regional Security Officers working in five overseas posts on issues related to consular staffing and resources, among other topics.

We visited U.S. consular posts in five countries—Brazil, the Dominican Republic, India, Jordan, and Ukraine. During these visits, we observed visa operations and interviewed consular staff and embassy management about visa adjudication policies, procedures, and resources. In addition, we spoke with officials from other U.S. agencies that assist consular officers in the visa adjudication process. We chose Brazil, the Dominican Republic, India, and Ukraine because each of the fraud prevention teams in these countries investigated 500 or more fraud cases in fiscal year 2010. We chose Jordan because of the nature of the fraud cases investigated in that country, which included security concerns.

We conducted our work from August 2011 through September 2012, in accordance with generally accepted government auditing standards. Those standards require that we plan and perform the audit to obtain sufficient, appropriate evidence to provide a reasonable basis for our findings and conclusions based on our audit objectives. We believe that the evidence obtained provides a reasonable basis for our findings and conclusions based on our audit objectives.

Appendix II. U.S. Nonimmigrant Visa Classes of Admission

Foreign nationals seeking to enter the United States temporarily may apply for entry under the following visa classes of admission:

Visa Class	Description
Transit aliens	
C-1	Aliens in continuous and immediate transit through the United States
C-2	Aliens in transit to the United Nations Headquarters District
C-3	Foreign government officials, attendants, servants, and personal employees, and spouses and children in transit
Temporary visitors for business	
B-1	Temporary visitors for business
GB	Visa Waiver Program—temporary visitors for business to Guam
WB	Visa Waiver Program—temporary visitors for business
Temporary visitors for pleasure	
B-2	Temporary visitors for pleasure
GT	Visa Waiver Program—temporary visitors for pleasure to Guam
WT	Visa Waiver Program—temporary visitors for pleasure
Temporary workers and trainees	
H-1B	Temporary workers with "specialty occupation"
H-1B1	Chile and Singapore Free Trade Agreement Aliens
H-1C	Nurses under the Nursing Relief for Disadvantaged Areas Act of 1999
H-2A	Seasonal agricultural workers
H-2B	Seasonal nonagricultural workers
H-3	Trainees
H-4	Spouses and children of H-1, H-2, or H-3 visa holders
O-1	Temporary workers with extraordinary ability or achievement in the sciences, arts, education, business, athletics, TV or film.
O-2	Temporary workers with essential skills accompanying and assisting O-1 visa holders
O-3	Spouses and children of O-1 and O-2 visa holders
P-1	Temporary workers—internationally recognized athletes or entertainers for a specific competition or performance
P-2	Temporary workers—artists or entertainers under reciprocal exchange programs with a similar organization of a foreign state

Visa Class	Description
P-3	Temporary workers—artists or entertainers under culturally unique programs
P-4	Spouses and children of P-1, P-2, or P-3 visa holders
Q-1	Temporary workers in international cultural exchange programs
R-1	Temporary workers in religious occupations
R-2	Spouses and children of R-1 visa holders
TN	North American Free Trade Agreement (NAFTA) professional workers
TD	Spouses and children of TN visa holders
Treaty traders and investors	
E-1	Treaty traders and spouses and children
E-2	Treaty investors and spouses and children
E-3	Australian Free Trade Agreement principals and spouses and children
Intracompany transferees	
L-1	Intracompany transferees
L-2	Spouses and children of L-1 visa holders
Representatives of foreign information media	
I-1	Representatives of foreign information media and spouses and children
Students	
F-1	Students—academic institutions
F-2	Spouses and children of F-1 visa holders
F-3	Canadian or Mexican national commuter students—academic institutions
M-1	Students—vocational/nonacademic institutions
M-2	Spouses and children of M-1 visa holders
M-3	Canadian or Mexican national commuter students—vocational/nonacademic institutions
Exchange visitors	
J-1	Exchange visitors
J-2	Spouses and children of J-1 visa holders
Other categories	
A-1	Ambassadors, public ministers, career diplomatic or consular officers, and spouses and children
A-2	Other foreign government officials or employees and spouses and children

(Continued)

Visa Class	Description
A-3	Attendants, servants, or personal employees of A-1 and A-2 visa holders and spouses and children
BE	Bering Strait Agreement aliens
FSM	Federated States of Micronesia nationals
G-1	Principal resident representatives of recognized foreign member governments to international organizations, staff, and spouses and children
G-2	Temporary representatives of recognized foreign member governments to international organizations and spouses and children
G-3	Representatives of unrecognized or nonmember foreign governments to international organizations and spouses and children
G-4	Officers or employees of unrecognized international organizations and spouses and children
G-5	Attendants, servants, or personal employees of G-1, G-2, G-3, or G-4 visa holders and spouses and children
K-1	Alien fiancés(ees) of U.S. citizens
K-2	Children of K-1 visa holders
K-3	Alien spouses of U.S. citizens
K-4	Children of K-3 visa holders
MIS	Republic of the Marshall Islands nationals
N-1 to N-7	North Atlantic Treaty Organization (NATO) aliens, spouses, and children
N-8	Parents of international organization special immigrants
N-9	Children of N-8 visa holders or international organization special immigrants
PAL	Republic of Palau nationals
Q-2	Irish Peace Process Cultural and Training Program aliens
Q-3	Spouses and children of Q-2 visa holders
T-1 to T-5	Victims of a severe form of trafficking and spouses, children, parents, and siblings
U-1 to U-4	Aliens suffering physical or mental abuse as victims of criminal activity and spouses, children, and parents
V-1 to V-3	Spouses and children of a lawful permanent resident who has been waiting 3 years or more for immigrant visas and dependents

Source: State.

APPENDIX III. CASE STUDIES

The following five case studies provide examples of the types of activities carried out by Fraud Prevention Units and Assistant Regional Security Officer Investigators (ARSO-Is) overseas.

Fraud Prevention Unit Case Study

In Ukraine, we observed consular officers adjudicating visas for the Summer Work and Travel program. A consular officer suspected an applicant's student identification was fraudulent, and he told the applicant to wait while he asked the Fraud Prevention Unit for assistance. The senior Locally Employed Staff (LES) person inspected the student ID and said it was most likely a fake. The consular officer asked the LES to assist in questioning the applicant. The LES reviewed the applicant's school transcripts that were submitted with the visa application, and asked the applicant to provide the name of the school's chancellor. The applicant could not provide the name. The Fraud Prevention Unit called the school to attempt to verify whether the applicant was currently enrolled, but the school would not verify the applicant's status. The Fraud Prevention Unit told the consular officer that they believed the applicant was committing fraud on her application, and the consular officer denied the visa.

ARSO-I Case Studies

U.S. Embassy Santo Domingo, the Dominican Republic

U.S. Major League Baseball (MLB) teams award large signing bonuses to younger prospective players in the Dominican Republic, creating a significant economic incentive to make prospective players seem younger. As a result, MLB prospects often falsify their ages and sometimes their identities on visa applications to make them appear younger than they truly are. To date, ARSO-I Santo Domingo has facilitated the arrests of two MLB Dominican talent scouts, an MLB Investigator, and an MLB pitcher, among others, for participating in identity fraud. The pitcher, a Dominican citizen, assumed the identity of a younger person and obtained a contract to play professional baseball as a pitcher in the United States in 1999. The pitcher has since illegally obtained at least 10 nonimmigrant visas in his assumed identity.

ARSO-I Santo Domingo confirmed the pitcher's true identity and coordinated with the Dominican prosecutors' office to obtain a Dominican arrest warrant. The pitcher later returned to the Dominican Republic and obtained travel documents and a new nonimmigrant visa petition from the MLB in his true identity, and applied for a nonimmigrant visa. The interviewing consular officer found the pitcher ineligible for the nonimmigrant visa due to identity fraud, and the ARSOI-I Santo Domingo subsequently facilitated his arrest by the Dominican National Police, based on his outstanding Dominican arrest warrant.

U.S. Consulate Sao Paulo, Brazil

In December 2010, Sao Paulo Civil Police arrested a Brazilian who presented false documents in support of his U.S. visa application. This was the ninth arrest of applicants whom had named the same individual known to be a smuggler and fraudulent document vender on their visa application. Further investigation identified approximately 70 persons who had used false documents provided by the document vendor since 2009. ARSO-I Sao Paulo received information that the document vendor and his accomplices were also producing false documents in support of Canadian visa applications, and Italian and Brazilian passports. In March 2011, the Brazilian Federal Police, the State of Santa Catarina Civil Police, and the State of Santa Catarina Prosecutor's office arrested the document vendor and three of his accomplices.

U.S. Embassy New Delhi, India

Immigrations Customs Enforcement (ICE) contacted the Deputy Assistant Regional Officer Investigator in New Delhi after receiving information that a private translator was extorting money from U.S. Citizenship and Immigration Services (USCIS) refugee/asylum applicants. The translator had access to protected information from USCIS files. ICE spoke with an informant who was being threatened by the translator to pay significant sums or have her application denied. Preliminary investigations determined that the translator would "cold-call" asylum applicants. ARSO-I New Delhi and ICE interviewed the translator, three USCIS local employees, and three local guards. The translator denied obtaining personal identifiable information from embassy staff. As a result of this investigation, the translator was arrested upon departure of the Embassy, one local guard was terminated for accepting money from the translator, and one USCIS LES employee was put on administrative leave for divulging personally identifiable information.

U.S. Embassy Kyiv, Ukraine

Immigration Customs Enforcement (ICE) Attaché contacted ARSO-I Kyiv for assistance with an individual present in Kyiv with an active INTERPOL Red Warrant for human trafficking. The fugitive was wanted in the Eastern District of Michigan for forced labor, money laundering, immigration and visa fraud, and witness tampering. ARSO-I Kyiv coordinated assistance with the Ministry of Internal Affairs Organized Crime Department. The Ukrainian Ministry of Internal Affairs Organized Crime Department agents arrested the fugitive at his residence for immigration overstay charges. ARSO-I Kyiv and ICE Attaché Frankfurt escorted the fugitive from Kyiv to New York, where the fugitive was arrested by ICE agents.

End Notes

[1] GAO, *Border Security: Strengthened Visa Process Would Benefit from Improvements in Staffing and Information Sharing*, GAO-05-859 (Washington, D.C.: Sept.13, 2005).

[2] GAO, *Border Security: Security of New Passports and Visas Enhanced, but More Needs to Be Done to Prevent Their Fraudulent Use*, GAO-07-1006 (Washington, D.C.: July 31, 2007).

[3] GAO, *Border Security: Fraud Risks Complicate State's Ability to Manage Diversity Visa Program*, GAO-07-1174 (Washington, D.C.: Sept. 21, 2007). The program provides up to 55,000 immigrant visas each fiscal year to aliens from countries with low rates of immigration to the United States. Diversity visas provide an immigration opportunity to individuals from such countries.

[4] The issuance of all visas is governed by the Immigration and Nationality Act of 1952 as amended by subsequent immigration legislation.

[5] See appendix III for specific case studies of the Fraud Prevention Unit and the Assistant Regional Security Officer Investigator.

[6] For more information on State staffing, see GAO, *Department of State: Foreign Service Midlevel Staffing Gaps Persist Despite Significant Increases in Hiring*, GAO-12-721 (Washington, D.C.: June 14, 2012).

[7] Not all consular posts have a dedicated Fraud Prevention Unit. Some posts are very small and provide limited consular services (such as only American Citizen Services, and no visa services).

[8] By the summer of 2013, Diplomatic Security plans to have 105 ARSO-Is working in 93 posts in 63 countries, according to Diplomatic Security officials.

[9] Diplomatic Security assigns ARSO-Is based on a number of factors including the number of visas adjudicated and visa refusal rates. At posts without an ARSO-I, the Diplomatic Security Regional Security Officer is responsible for criminal investigations of visa fraud. However, Regional Security Officers have numerous responsibilities, such as physical security of the compound, and according to State officials are not able to dedicate a large portion of their time to investigating visa fraud.

[10] For more information on the Visa Security Program, see GAO, *Border Security: DHS's Visa Security Program Needs to Improve Performance Evaluation and Better Address Visa Risk Worldwide*, GAO-11-315 (Washington, D.C.: Mar. 31, 2011).

[11] KCC is a centralized nonimmigrant and diversity visa processing facility. The National Visa Center is a centralized immigrant visa processing facility.

[12] The Consular Consolidated Database contains passport, nonimmigrant visa, and immigrant visa application information that has been collected since 1999.
[13] These data include border crossing cards issued to Mexican nationals.
[14] Approximately 775,000 of the 2.1 million refusals were waived or overcome in fiscal year 2011. The Immigration and Nationality Act contains provisions that may allow a visa applicant who was denied a visa for a particular ineligibility to apply for a waiver of that ineligibility. DHS adjudicates all waivers of immigrant and nonimmigrant visa ineligibility. Waivers are discretionary, meaning that there are no guarantees that DHS will approve a waiver. If the waiver is approved, the applicant can be issued a visa. For nonimmigrant visa waivers, the consular officer must first choose to recommend to DHS that the applicant be considered for a waiver.
[15] Visa applicants who are deemed ineligible and refused nonimmigrant visas may apply, and State may choose to overcome the initial refusal or the applicant may apply for a waiver. The information in table 1 depicts adjusted refusal rates based on both overcomes and waivers.
[16] Under section 214(b) of the Immigration and Nationality Act,[8 U.S.C. 1184(b)], an applicant for a nonimmigrant visa is generally presumed to be an intending immigrant until the applicant can demonstrate to the satisfaction of an interviewing consular officer that they are entitled to the type of visa for which they are applying and that they will depart the United States at the end of their authorized temporary stay.
[17] An applicant who, by fraud or willful misrepresentation of a material fact, attempts to obtain a visa or admission into the United States is inadmissible under section 212(a)(6)(C)(i) of the Immigration and Nationality Act.
[18] For U.S. citizens petitioning for a family member, immediate relatives include spouses, parents of citizens ages 21 and older, and citizens' unmarried children under age 21. There is no limit on the number of immediate relatives of U.S. citizens that can seek lawful permanent residency. U.S. citizens may also petition for adult children and for siblings; and there are numerical limits on these categories. For lawful permanent residents petioning for a family member, the family member must be a spouse, a child or an unmarried adult son or daughter; and there are numerical limits.
[19] Permanent residency based on employment may be provided to aliens such as (1) professionals with advanced degrees, (2) persons with exceptional ability, (3) skilled or professional workers, (4) special immigrants, and (5) immigrant investors. Immigration law limits the annual number of employer-sponsored immigrants.
[20] The DS-260 is an online immigrant visa form that is replacing the DS-230, a paper form. State is in the process of rolling out the DS-260 around the world, according to State officials.
[21] In June 2005, State's Office of Fraud Prevention Programs developed a one-time fraud ranking of posts that included weighted criteria based on demographics, immigrant and nonimmigrant visa refusal rates, DHS statistics on adjustments of status by country, posts' own assessments of fraud, and a country corruption index. This one-time ranking was primarily used to assist in deliberations on ARSO-I placement.
[22] State's suspected and confirmed fraud case data for fiscal year 2011 were divided into two data systems, and some cases may have been double-counted. We determined that State's data for fiscal year 2010 were more reliable for our purposes.
[23] These countries have many fraud cases because they process a high volume of visas.
[24] The most common of these types of visas are H and L visas. H visas are for temporary workers and L visas are for intracompany transfers. In 2011, 56 percent of all skilled worker visas (H-1B) were issued to citizens of India and 94 percent of all temporary agricultural visas (H-2A) were issued to citizens of Mexico. For more information, see *Visa Program: Reforms Are Needed to Minimize the Risks and Costs of Current Program*, GAO-11-26 (Washington, D.C.: Jan. 14, 2011).
[25] As a result of the findings of this study and others, USCIS launched an Administrative Site Visit and Verification Program (ASVVP) —an ongoing program to visit work sites of

companies hiring skilled workers and considered to be at a higher risk for abusing the program, according to officials. All H1-B ASVVP cases are randomly selected. During fiscal year 2010, USCIS conducted 14,433 skilled worker visa site inspections, which resulted in 948 adverse actions, such as the revocation or denial of benefits, or the referral of a case for criminal investigation.

[26] H-1B Visa Reform Act of 2004, Pub. L. No. 108-447, Div. J, Title IV, Section 426, 118 Stat. 3357. In addition, legislation established an additional fee of $2,000 for petitions filed through September 30, 2015, for petitioners with 50 or more employees in the United States and more than 50 percent of those U.S. employees on H-1B or L visas. Pub. L. No. 111-230, § 402(b), 123 Stat. 2485, 2487, as amended by Publ. L. No 111-347, § 302, Jan. 2, 2011, 124 Stat. 3667.

[27] Students are granted F and M visas. F visas are for study at academic institutions and M visas are for study at vocational or nonacademic institutions. According to State's regulations, a student visa applicant must meet the following requirements to qualify: (1) acceptance at an approved school; (2) possession of sufficient funds; (3) sufficient knowledge of the English language to undertake the chosen course of study or training (unless coming to participate exclusively in an English language training program); and (4) present intent to leave the United States at conclusion of studies. See 22 C.F.R. § 41.61(b)(1) and 8 U.S.C. § 1101(a)(15)(F) and § 1101(a)(15)(M).

[28] For more information, see GAO, *Student and Exchange Visitor Program, DHS Needs to Assess Risks and Strengthen Oversight Functions,* GAO-12-572 (Washington, D.C.: June 18, 2012).

[29] Exchange visitors are granted J visas. J visas do not involve petitioners, and are therefore not screened in the same manner as petition-based applications, according to State officials.

[30] See 77 Fed. Reg. 27593 to be codified at 22 C.F.R. PART 62.

[31] Immigration Act of 1990, Pub. L. No. 101-649, § 131, 104 Stat. 4978, 4997-99 (1990) (codified at 8 U.S.C. § 1153 (c).

[32] In fiscal year 2011, between 5,000 and 6,000 individuals were registered for diversity visas from Bangladesh, Ethiopia, Ghana, Nigeria, and Ukraine.

[33] The other six countries among State's 2005 Fraud Ranking included: Bangladesh, El Salvador, Haiti, Honduras, Nigeria, and the Philippines.

[34] MATRIX stands for Match Analytics and Trusted Real-Time Identity X-Ref (or cross-reference).

[35] The International Criminal Police Organization (INTERPOL) is the world's largest international police organization that helps police understand criminal trends, analyze information, conduct operations and, ultimately, arrest as many criminals as possible, according to INTERPOL's website.

[36] Visa referrals occur when State officials refer their professional contacts for expedited visa appointments, reducing their wait time for scheduling an interview with a consular officer.

[37] Since 2008, State has been given access to DHS's Arrival and Departure Information System (ADIS) to generate a sample of issued visas to conduct a validation study. In 2011, ADIS results were linked to each visa application so that consular officers could view applicants' prior travel history.

[38] In addition to the contractors, State employs two Foreign Service Officers, two Civil Service employees, one Diplomatic Security Special Agent, and five assistants. DHS employs one Fraud Detection National Security Directorate staff member, according to KCC officials.

[39] KCC employees do not make decisions on whether or not to issue a visa.

[40] The consular component of State's Overseas Staffing Model uses consular workload and environmental factors to assist in the allocation of staffing resources. Workload factors include the number of immigrant, nonimmigrant, and diversity visa cases processed annually, and environmental factors include fraud and the number of third-country national applications processed, among other criteria.

[41] Although State provided us with the parameters of five KCC pilots, it was unable to provide the results of each pilot.

[42] When a post requests additional KCC assistance, KCC officials must consult with the Visa Office, in coordination with the Office of Fraud Prevention Programs, before initiating the service.

[43] The George P. Shultz National Foreign Affairs Training Center's Foreign Service Institute is the federal government's primary training institution for officers and support personnel of the U.S. foreign affairs community.

[44] The Foreign Service Institute also offers PC542, a fraud prevention course for locally employed staff.

[45] State's survey reached 158 of the 222 visa-issuing consular posts. We determined the results to be sufficiently reliable for our purposes.

[46] The lack of training is a trend that has continued since at least 2005, when we reported that 10 of the 25 consular managers with whom we met said that their Fraud Prevention Managers had not yet received training specific to their fraud prevention duties.

[47] In March 2009, a GAO investigation exposed major vulnerabilities in State's passport issuance process, demonstrating that terrorists or criminals could steal an American citizen's identity, use basic counterfeiting skills to create fraudulent documentation for that identity, and obtain a genuine U.S. passport. GAO, *Department of State: Undercover Tests Reveal Significant Vulnerabilities in State's Passport Issuance Process*, GAO-09-447 (Washington, D.C.: Mar. 13, 2009).

INDEX

#

9/11, 21, 23, 24, 25
9/11 Commission, 21

A

abuse, 64
access, 8, 15, 18, 20, 23, 45, 46, 51, 52, 53, 58, 66, 69
accountability, 55
adjustment, 4
administrative support, 20
admission criteria, vii, 1, 2
Africa, 45
age, vii, 1, 6, 7, 68
agencies, 3, 11, 12, 14, 15, 30, 34, 35, 61
algorithm, 11
alien smuggling, 34
aliens, vii, viii, 1, 2, 3, 4, 5, 6, 7, 8, 11, 13, 23, 32, 40, 45, 58, 62, 64, 67, 68
appointments, 69
arrest(s), 34, 50, 65, 66, 69
Asia, 43
assessment, 37, 41
asylum, 4, 46, 66
athletes, 62
Attorney General, 5, 21
audit, 31, 61
authorities, vii, 1, 6, 7, 18
authority, 6, 13, 14, 15, 18, 19, 20, 21, 31, 40
awareness, 20

B

Bangladesh, 69
Beijing, 54
beneficiaries, 51
benefits, 35, 37, 46, 53, 69
biographic data, vii, 1, 2, 8
biometric, vii, 1, 2, 8, 18, 25, 40, 57
birth certificates, vii, 1, 6, 7, 40
bonuses, 65
border crossing, 37, 68
border inspections, 22
Border Patrol, 41
border security, vii, 1, 2, 31, 32
Brazil, 28, 35, 36, 37, 41, 42, 61, 66
businesses, 44

C

cables, 48, 49
Cairo, 15
case studies, 65, 67
CBP, 3, 5, 8, 22, 23
CCD, vii, 2, 8, 12, 23
certificate, 40
certification, 7, 9

chain of command, 20
children, 62, 63, 64, 68
Chile, 62
China, 15, 28, 35, 36, 37, 41, 42, 54
citizens, 19, 31, 45, 53, 64, 68
citizenship, 7, 45
classes, 4, 15, 19, 62
classification, 13
classroom, 55
clients, 46
collaboration, 20
Colombia, 54
commercial, 20
Committees on Appropriations, 24
communication, 53
community, 70
compensation, 19
competition, 62
complement, 15
Congress, 3, 16, 17, 18, 21, 22, 23, 24, 25
Consular Consolidated Database, vii, 2, 8, 23, 35, 37, 42, 47, 48, 59, 68
consulting, 16
content analysis, 55
cooperation, 41
coordination, 49, 70
corruption, 41, 68
counterfeiting, 70
counterterrorism, 13, 15, 30, 55
covering, 55
crimes, viii, 27, 30, 58
criminal activity, 33, 41, 64
criminal investigations, 33, 50, 67
criminals, 3, 69, 70
culture, 33
Customs and Border Protection, 3, 35

D

damages, iv
data collection, 61
data mining, 51
database, vii, 2, 5, 8, 11, 23, 50, 57, 61
demonstrations, 60
denial, 19, 69

Department of Agriculture, 21
Department of Health and Human Services, 21
Department of Homeland Security, 2, 17, 24, 25, 29, 32
Department of Justice, 21
Department of Labor, 4, 21
depth, 16
detection, 32, 34, 43, 55
DHS, 2, 5, 8, 11, 15, 17, 18, 19, 20, 21, 23, 24, 25, 29, 32, 34, 35, 43, 59, 67, 68, 69
direct mail, 48
distance learning, 28, 56, 59
distribution, 52
diversity, 4, 40, 41, 43, 45, 49, 50, 67, 69
DOL, 21
Dominican Republic, 28, 41, 42, 46, 54, 61, 65
draft, 59
Drug Enforcement Administration (DEA), 11
DS-1, 39, 40, 47, 51
due process, 24

E

earnings, 5
Eastern Europe, 45
education, 62
Egypt, 15
El Salvador, 69
eligibility criteria, 6
embassy, 40, 43, 61, 66
employees, 15, 20, 50, 51, 62, 63, 64, 66, 69
employers, 9, 51
employment, 42, 51, 68
enforcement, 14, 16, 18, 34
enrollment, 29, 55, 58, 60
entertainers, 62, 63
environment, 16, 41
environmental factors, 69
ethics, 55
evidence, 9, 10, 11, 12, 31, 40, 47, 50, 61
evolution, 59
examinations, vii, 1, 6, 7

exclusion, 7, 10, 23
Executive Order, 37
exercise, 19
expertise, 15, 33

F

facilitators, 45
family members, 22
FBI, 11, 13, 23
Federal Bureau of Investigation (FBI), 8
federal government, 70
Federal Register, 24
financial, 5, 37, 44
fingerprints, vii, 1, 7, 8, 23, 40, 43, 50
flexibility, 33, 47
force, 14
foreign affairs, 70
Foreign nationals, vii, viii, 1, 2, 7, 27, 62
foreign person, 50
foreign policy, 13, 19, 34
funds, 69

G

GAO, viii, 24, 25, 27, 28, 29, 36, 37, 39, 44, 55, 67, 68, 69, 70
General Accounting Office, 24
globalization, 41, 46
governments, 17, 64
Guangzhou, 53, 54
guidance, 34, 41, 49, 60

H

Haiti, 69
health, 7, 21, 44
HHS, 21
hiring, 9, 30, 69
history, 7, 10, 47, 69
homeland security, 17, 19
Homeland Security Act, 15, 17, 18, 25
Honduras, 69
Hong Kong, 15

host, 16, 33
House, 16, 23, 24
human, viii, 27, 30, 34, 46, 67

I

ICE, 15, 20, 29, 34, 35, 66, 67
ID, 65
identification, 34, 65
identity, viii, 20, 27, 30, 65, 70
immigrants, 4, 30, 45, 64, 68
immigration, vii, 1, 2, 3, 5, 7, 15, 16, 18, 19, 21, 22, 24, 35, 37, 45, 49, 67
Immigration Act, 3, 21, 45, 69
Immigration and Customs Enforcement(ICE), 3, 15, 23, 24, 25, 29, 34
Immigration and Nationality Act, 3, 4, 18, 21, 24, 67, 68
Impact Assessment, 23
improvements, 21, 49, 50
inadmissible, 18, 68
income, 9
incubator, 51
India, 28, 35, 36, 37, 41, 42, 43, 46, 51, 53, 54, 61, 66, 68
individuals, 13, 36, 45, 46, 67, 69
industry, 30, 37
information technology, 46
injury, iv
INS, 20
inspections, 18, 22, 69
inspectors, 5, 23
institutions, 63, 69
integration, 16
integrity, viii, 2, 3, 27, 33, 58
intelligence, 12, 13, 14, 35
Intelligence Reform and Terrorism Prevention Act, 21
Internal Revenue Service, 5
investors, 63, 68
Islamabad, 15
issues, 16, 17, 25, 30, 31, 34, 57, 61

Index

J

Jamaica, 46
Jordan, 61
jurisdiction, 15, 34

L

law enforcement, 8, 12, 13, 14, 15, 16, 20, 34, 35, 41
lawful permanent residents, vii, 1, 68
laws, 18, 19, 34
lead, 17, 34
Leahy, 24
legislation, 3, 16, 24, 67, 69
LPRs, vii, 1, 4, 6, 7, 9, 10

M

Major League Baseball, 30, 65
majority, 42, 52, 53, 56, 58
management, 28, 29, 32, 50, 52, 53, 60, 61
manipulation, 30
marriage, vii, 1, 6, 7, 45, 46
Marshall Islands, 64
matter, iv
media, 63
medical, 40
methodology, 31
Mexico, 28, 35, 36, 37, 41, 42, 46, 54, 68
mission(s), viii, 2, 3, 22, 31
money laundering, 67
Morocco, 15
Moscow, 46

N

NAFTA, 63
narcotics, 30
National Counterterrorism Center (NCTC), 12
National Crime Information Center, 20
national security, viii, 2, 3, 35

nationality, 3, 18, 19
NATO, 64
NCTC, 13
Nigeria, 69
noncitizens, 4
North America, 63
North American Free Trade Agreement, 63
North Atlantic Treaty Organization, 64

O

Office of Management and Budget, 37
officials, vii, viii, 12, 14, 16, 21, 27, 28, 31, 33, 34, 41, 42, 43, 44, 45, 48, 49, 50, 51, 53, 56, 57, 59, 60, 61, 62, 63, 67, 68, 69, 70
operations, viii, 20, 28, 34, 61, 69
opportunities, 33
oversight, 34

P

Pakistan, 15
parents, 64, 68
parole, 21
participants, 5, 45
permission, iv
permit, 14
Peru, 46
Philippines, 15, 69
photographs, viii, 2, 8, 50, 56
planning decisions, 53
playing, 17
pleasure, 62
police, 69
policy, viii, 2, 3, 16, 19, 21, 28, 34, 46, 53, 58, 59
port of entry, 3, 4, 5, 41
preparation, iv
President, 37
President Obama, 37
prevention, vii, viii, 27, 28, 31, 32, 34, 43, 46, 47, 49, 55, 56, 57, 58, 59, 60, 61, 70
professionals, 68

project, 50
public health, viii, 2, 3
public safety, 35

Q

questioning, 65

R

reciprocity, 17, 19
recognition, 8, 33, 50
recommendations, 21, 28, 50, 59
reform, 9, 12, 16, 18, 23, 24, 69
refugee status, 4
refugees, 4
regulations, 6, 14, 15, 18, 19, 69
relatives, 68
reliability, 41, 59, 60, 61
relief, 4
requirements, vii, viii, 3, 5, 18, 21, 27, 28, 31, 59, 60, 69
resolution, 21
resources, vii, viii, 15, 27, 28, 30, 31, 42, 46, 49, 53, 57, 58, 59, 60, 61, 69
response, 28
rights, iv
rings, 46
risk(s), 15, 34, 35, 49, 69
risk profile, 15
rules, 44

S

safety, viii, 2, 3, 14, 23, 44
Saudi Arabia, 15, 20
school, 43, 65, 69
scope, 19, 31
Secretary of Homeland Security, 19, 21, 34
secure communication, 12
security, vii, viii, 2, 3, 7, 15, 16, 17, 19, 20, 21, 23, 30, 33, 34, 35, 40, 46, 55, 58, 61, 67
security threats, 15, 34

Senate, 3, 16, 22, 23, 24, 25, 30
Senate Committee on the Judiciary, 3, 16, 22, 24, 25
September 11, 18, 30, 35, 50
services, 28, 48, 51, 53, 57, 58, 67
sibling(s), 4, 64, 68
Singapore, 62
skilled workers, 69
smuggling, 46
software, 50, 56
South Asia, 45
specific knowledge, 17
specifications, 5
staffing, 17, 52, 61, 67, 69
state, 18, 23, 24, 35, 62
statistics, viii, 28, 52, 68
statutes, 3
subscribers, 49
supervisors, 20

T

talent, 65
Task Force, 35
teams, 61, 65
technical comments, 59
techniques, 20, 49
technologies, vii, viii, 27, 28, 31, 46, 58, 59, 60
technology, 8, 21, 41, 46, 49, 56
terrorism, viii, 27, 30
terrorist attack, 18, 35
terrorists, 8, 12, 17, 32, 58, 70
Test of English as a Foreign Language, 43
The Homeland Security Act, 18
threats, 13, 16
Title I, 69
Title IV, 69
TOEFL, 43
tourism, 17, 35, 37
tracks, 8
trade, 17
trafficking, viii, 27, 30, 34, 46, 64, 67
trainees, 62

training, vii, viii, 15, 16, 18, 19, 20, 21, 27, 28, 29, 30, 31, 32, 34, 49, 50, 55, 56, 57, 58, 59, 60, 69, 70
training programs, 56
transcripts, 65
transmission, 15
travel documents, viii, 27, 30, 35, 66
Treasury, 20
triggers, 13

U

U.S. economy, viii, 2, 3, 37
Ukraine, 54, 61, 65, 67, 69
United Nations, 62
United States, v, vii, viii, 1, 2, 3, 4, 5, 7, 8, 9, 10, 14, 18, 19, 21, 22, 23, 25, 27, 28, 30, 32, 35, 36, 40, 42, 43, 44, 45, 46, 48, 49, 58, 62, 65, 67, 68, 69
USDA, 21

V

validation, 48, 49, 69

Venezuela, 15
venue, 52
victims, 64
violence, viii, 27, 30
visa applicant, vii, 1, 2, 6, 7, 8, 11, 13, 15, 16, 17, 28, 36, 37, 40, 42, 44, 46, 48, 50, 52, 58, 68, 69
visa issuance process, vii, 1, 2, 5, 18, 30
visa system, 33
Visa Waiver Program, 5, 21, 22, 62

W

waiver, 68
Washington, 13, 57, 67, 68, 69, 70
web, 40, 49
welfare, 44
workers, 5, 9, 22, 43, 62, 63, 68
workload, 28, 32, 46, 50, 52, 58, 59, 69
World Trade Center, 12
World War I, 3
worldwide, 34, 36, 42, 47, 49, 50, 51, 58